Dearest Finn & Bjørn

This book is for you.
You light our fire!

—Mom & Dad

COOKING ON FIRE

NICOLAI & EVA TRAM

gestalten

CONTENTS

INTRODUCTION

For decades, open-fire cooking has been considered a pastime reserved for scouts and elite soldiers, leaving the rest of us to grill sausages on the terrace. But open-fire cooking is for everyone. It is sensuous and impractical in the best sense of the word. It is as much about the time spent making the food as it is about eating it.

Since man discovered the art of controlling fire a million years ago, and well into the age of industrialization, fire has had various practical functions. It is what allowed us to venture out of Africa, and why people are able to live in Northern climates at all today. Fire gave us heat, security, and allowed us to prepare our food in a whole new way. When we settled down as farmers, we brought fire into our homes and made it a daily part of our lives until the years after World War II. But since then, woodburning stoves and fire have slid further and further into the shadows of the past. In the modern Western world, we no longer need an open fire close at hand to meet our basic needs. The fire, which once lit up our lives, has finally dwindled. Sure, we may light campfires when we want things to be really cozy or the odd candle when we have guests over. But when it comes down to it, fire no longer has a necessary role to play in our lives ... or does it?

We live in a time when we humans have fewer and fewer opportunities to put our brains on pause. We're constantly running around with a plethora of tasks that need to be completed, errands that need to be run, and incoming information that needs to be processed, all vying for our attention at once. Time we previously spent staring off into space is now spent listening to a podcast or reading the news. Time that used to be spent in silence is filled up with the noise of our smartphone activities and televisions, which in turn give us even more information to process. Very rarely do we find ourselves in environments with changing but calm stimuli that fascinate us and require no targeted attention, where we can truly empty our minds. For example, do you remember when, as a child, you would lie on the ground just watching the clouds go by? Those clouds are still there.

But for most of us adults, it would feel wrong to lie on the ground looking up at the clouds. It is, after all, unproductive, useless, and rarely something we can do with a good conscience. But with fire, the relaxed feeling arises automatically, and it is our mission to make you prioritize it. You cannot rush a campfire. Open-fire cooking is not something you do at the last minute. It requires that you are always one step ahead, and that is a good thing.

Because if there is one thing we would like to accomplish with this book, it is to give you, the reader, the freedom to sit down by the fire, and with food as the excuse, look into the flames, and truly relax. In this sense, this is perhaps the first cookbook where the food is not the primary focus. The primary ingredient in this cookbook is you. Campfires are great at cooking delicious food, but they are also valuable spiritual sustenance. We firmly believe that the peace that arises from gazing into the flames of an open fire cannot be found anywhere else.

We hope you will enjoy our book.

—Eva H. Tram & Nicolai Tram

COOKING WITH FIRE

Open fire cooking is a discipline on par with any other kind of cooking—French, Italian, New Nordic, or anything else you could think of. One thing you quickly discover when you start cooking with fire is that it is, first and foremost, highly impractical. It is something one must learn to master. But that is also the fun of it, that there are always so many new things to learn—about the food, but also about yourself. You should consider cooking with fire as an organic process: as a collaboration between you and the fire. That is part of the charm. But that is not to say that you should jump into it without any kind of introduction. Once equipped with the tools this book provides you, you will have a greater, more balanced synergy with the fire, and the confidence of knowing that you are always able to tame it.

WHEN IS THE BEST TIME TO COOK WITH FIRE?

Cooking with fire is not just a summer thing. Of course, it makes perfect sense to build a campfire in the summer when you are outdoors anyway. But we really think it's an art that should be practiced all year round. Unlike a barbecue grill, the heat from a fire makes it possible to stay outdoors for hours without freezing, even in the coldest weather. Therefore, it is a great opportunity to spend time outside during cooler months. This book has been created over the course of a year, and to us, all seasons have their charm, in terms of both their unique produce and scenery.

WHY DOES FIRE-COOKED FOOD TASTE SO GOOD?

The fact that food cooked over open fire tastes better (or at least different) than food cooked over gas, an induction cooktop, or barbecue charcoal essentially comes down to two things: Maillard reactions and smoke. Maillard reactions and smoke are, of course, components of many other cooking techniques too. But it is the combination of these two natural, basic conditions for food cooked over an open fire that creates the distinctive taste unique to fire-cooked food.

The Maillard reaction

Fire cooking causes a smooth and dense Maillard reaction, the chemical reaction that takes place between amino acids and carbohydrates in our food when it is heated to over 250°F (120°C), making it dark and tasty. Prepared food has been an essential component of the intellectual and physical development of the human race. It has given us an advantage over other animals, which have to spend hours and hours chewing and digesting food. This advantage has been beneficial for our evolution, and that is why our bodies immediately reward us when we taste cooked food by triggering endorphins in our brains. It does so because it instinctively associates the taste of Maillard-browned foods with energy that can be quickly absorbed and digested.

Smoke

Wood consists of three primary components: cellulose, hemicellulose, and lignin. There are a number of other compounds too, but don't worry about them for now. When cellulose and hemicellulose burn, they slowly caramelize into sugar molecules, which creates a sweet aroma. And the same thing happens with the lignin, which is converted into various kinds of aromatics, such as vanillin, which also creates a distinct aroma. The smoke from the campfire permeates the food and enhances the taste and overall aroma. It takes the meal to another level, which cannot be replicated in a kitchen. This applies to the smoke from the wood that the various gases create when they escape the fire. And when the juice from the food drips down onto the embers and itself turns into smoke, the taste and aromas intensify further.

The inexplicable aspect

Last but not least, there is the sensuous aspect of fire. A quality that, on paper, should not have an influence on taste, but which it seems to have all the same. This is what happens when you are taken out of your kitchen—and here I do not mean out on the terrace to flip sausages on the grill. But down to earth, with smoke in your eyes and a smile on your face. To the place that is simultaneously relaxing and out of your comfort zone. When you are forced out of your comfort zone a miraculous and inexplicable thing happens: you can taste that something has been at stake. Food cooked over fire has a certain *je ne sais quoi* that food created in perfectly controlled environments can never replicate.

EQUIPMENT

It is a good idea to consider where you want to prepare your produce and ingredients before heading off to the fire. Generally speaking, you need to pay extra attention to hygiene, as you'll be working in an environment that is not as clean as your regular kitchen. Make sure to bring plenty of wet wipes out to the campfire. They're great to have at hand when you have no running water close by. The same goes for bowls and cutting boards. You can easily do your preparation inside your kitchen with handy features like a sink and dishwasher available, then take the food out to the fire to cook. But that's all up to you.

If you're a stickler for equipment, it can be easy to overspend on fancy gadgets and gizmos that you don't necessarily need. Of course, it is entirely up to you how much you want to splash out on equipment. But if you are a beginner, I recommend taking things one step at a time. You don't need to invest in braziers and cast-iron paraphernalia to get started. The most important thing is that you get out and learn how to work with the fire. Then, as you become more confident and ambitious, you can gradually introduce more tools into the mix. In fact, you probably already have most of the things you need or will easily be able to make them. On the next few pages, you can see what equipment I have obtained or made myself along the way.

1
26
4
8
9
7
3
2
6
5

20
23
21
25
24
19
22
18
10
11
13
15
16
14
12
17

1. Grill rack The more the merrier. I have three to four different racks that I use for different foods and techniques. Those with a wide surface area and thick grills are great for meat. Others, which have thinner grills and a smaller surface area, I use for vegetables, fish, and seafood.

2. Campfire stand A campfire stand can be easily made using three sticks, and a chain or a bit of string to hold the sticks together. You can also buy a premade stand. In some places, they are sold as a brazier/stand combo, which is great to have on the terrace.

3. Barbecue tongs A good, long set of barbecue tongs is always handy for adjusting the fire if it starts to burn unevenly or collapses prematurely.

4. Cord It can be convenient to tie up your food with a (flax) cord, which will help retain the moisture inside your ingredients, and make it easier to turn them over without them falling apart. I use the cord for meat and poultry, but also for more porous vegetables. Additionally, the cord can be used to make campfire stands and to hang various produce over the embers.

5. Grill brush It is important to keep your grill rack clean so you don't contaminate your fresh food with old roasted leftovers. I do not clean the grill rack when I am done cooking, but wait until I need to use it again. Then I leave the grill rack on the campfire and let it get very hot so that grease and food residue is charred and can be easily brushed off. Usually, I rub it with half a lemon (sliced-side down) afterward, which gets rid of any undesirable remnants.

6. Axe A good axe is absolutely indispensable. Use it before you start your campfire to split the firewood into kindling, and to prepare your spears and Y-sticks.

7. Tweezers A pair of kitchen tweezers is great for tossing and turning the food, and for moving small pieces of embers around your fire.

8. Camping knife The camping knife is a superb tool, as a knife for cooking, a tool for cutting the bark of the wood before lighting the fire, and for cutting small sticks off the firewood. I also use my camping knife to ignite my fire steel (a total no-no if you want to take care of your knife—but hey, nobody's perfect).

9. Fire steel A small magnesium rod that sends a 5,500°F (3,000°C) spark directly to your tinder when hit with the included plate or another piece of metal you have at hand. The fire steel is far more effective than matches, especially in wet weather conditions.

10. Leatherman An all-in-one multi-tool. You will mainly be using the pliers, scissors, and knife. A Leatherman is absolutely indispensable for tying meat and fish to your skewers, and it is handy because it takes up next to no space.

11. Copper wire Along with pliers, copper wire, or other metal wire that does not leave a metallic taste, ensures that the food you tie onto large skewers ends up in your stomach rather than on the ground. When dealing with large, heavy produce, you can feel confident relying on copper wire.

12. Y-sticks These are super practical and completely free, because they are provided by nature itself. You can use the same stick numerous times. They are great for supporting and fixing heavy spears, and can play a supporting role in your homebuilt rotisserie.

13. Ember shovel A small shovel is handy for distributing and moving the embers—for example, in a keyhole campfire, from the parent fire to the ember bench.

14. Rotisserie You can make a rotisserie yourself with two Y-sticks and a skewer. However, with time, you'll probably find yourself tempted to invest in a "real" rotisserie. The one I have is an old French mechanical type from the 18th century, which is handy because it doesn't require any power. But you can easily find newer models on the Web.

15. Flambadou The flambadou is used in an old method of cooking, dating back to the Middle Ages. The flambadou, which resembles a large candle extinguisher with a hole in the bottom, is placed in the embers until it is glowing hot, after which grease or lard is added and ignited. Flaming drops now fall from the little hole in the bottom, leaving your food crispy and with a lovely smoky flavor. I had my flambadou forged by Mikkel Blacksmith at Lejre Land of Legends in Denmark, but I have heard that you can buy them online too.

16. Coarse mesh sieves Flat and curved. They can be used as pans and saucepans for raw ingredients that are too small or thin for the grill but you'd like to have close to the smoke.

17. Pizza trowel A pizza trowel is handy for moving and turning flatbread and pizza. In addition, it can be used as a fan if the fire needs more oxygen.

18. Pitchfork A pitchfork is quite useful for restructuring a hot fire without getting too close to the flames or heat.

19. Cast-iron campfire pan A thick, heavy pan with legs provides an even heat distribution, which means you won't have the problem of burnt food in one half of your pan and raw food in the other.

20. Cloth A cloth has several uses. You can wrap up pots or food to keep them warm, use the cloth as a cover in your dirt oven, or use it to stifle your fire if it gets out of hand.

21. *Æbleskiver* pan *Æbleskiver* is a traditional Danish dessert cooked in a cast-iron pan with holes in it, which is mainly used for, well, *æbleskiver.* It isn't an especially necessary part of your toolkit, but if you come across one at a flea market, buy it!

22. Dutch oven If you're going to buy just one thing before you start cooking with fire, it should be a Dutch oven: a cast-iron pot with legs, a lid, and a handle. It has numerous uses. For example, you can use it as a pot, a pan, an oven, to hang things on, or it can stand directly in the embers. It is so sturdy and reliable, that if you take good care of it your grandchildren will be able to use it years from now.

23. Waffle iron There is a world of difference between waffles baked over fire and waffles baked on an electric waffle iron. You'll never want to go back to your standard, run-of-the-mill waffles once you've experienced the texture and flavor of waffles cooked on an open fire. Besides, hot waffles will surely lure even the most reserved family members out to the campfire.

24. *Råd* iron *Gode råd* is a type of cookie popular in Scandinavia in the 19th century, and at Danish flea markets there are always a couple of *gode råd* irons for sale. Again, absolutely noncompulsory, but nice to have.

25. Heat-resistant gloves A nice, thick pair of heat-resistant gloves lets you reach directly into the embers and are really nice to have when working close to the heat.

26. Grill net An inexpensive tool that's super useful for cooking fish, meat, and vegetables. It allows you to get your food close to the embers while keeping the ingredients together inside the net.

ABOUT OUR RECIPES

We have been as accurate as possible when writing up our recipes. However, it is important that you use them more as a guide and an inspiration than an infallible list of instructions. You can never achieve the same level of control over an open fire as you can over your oven or stove. There are simply too many variables. Wind and weather conditions, types of wood, how dry it is, how the fire is built, how well-lit it is. All of this has an impact on the outcome. With so many variables, it is essential that you let your own intuition and enthusiasm guide you. That you see, smell, taste, hear, and notice the food that is in your hands. It does not really matter if you add a few grams more or less of something, or whether you cook something for a minute over or under the guidelines. It will be delicious anyway.

I recommend that you read the next few pages before jumping into the recipes. Here you will find descriptions of the different types of firewood, campfires, and techniques needed to get the best out of the recipes. All the recipes are developed specifically for the campfire, where the technique used, the smoke, or the heat intensity is factored into the equation. Because, in my opinion, cooking with fire is not about preparing your usual kitchen-based meals with a nice natural backdrop. The true beauty lies in preparing meals that cannot be recreated indoors. I have deliberately refrained from putting together full meals in this book. Instead, I have chosen to list the dishes as individual components, which can be mixed and matched as you please to form a wonderful meal unique to you and your tastes. In other words, you will not find the recipe for a steak with a specific sauce, a potato dish, or a set of vegetables. Instead, you will find a number of elements that you can combine as you see fit. For the same reason, I do not work with starters or main courses in this book. Instead, I have chosen to divide the recipes into vegetables, seafood, meat, and sweets. It all fits together, so to speak, and there are no rules or requirements on what to pair with what. Allow your creativity, intuition, and common sense to take the lead. The same applies for the number of servings for each course. The amount of food in each dish depends entirely on how many guests you're serving and how hungry you are.

Last, I should remind you that it is also important to make room for mistakes. Embrace that food is actually at its best when it is not perfect. It is in its imperfections that your food becomes alive, authentic, and genuine. I strongly urge you to replace the pursuit of perfection with a laissez-faire attitude and love for the food and the people you are making it for. This is also how the dishes in this book have come into being.

In the recipes you will come across the following icons:

Type of fire

Campfire strength

Equipment

ABOUT THE CAMPFIRE

How you build your campfire matters if you want a good result. Some campfires provide more protection from the wind, some provide powerful direct heat, some are good for producing embers, and others for developing smoke. Therefore, the first thing you need to consider is what kind of dish you are going to make. Then you can start building the most effective fire for your choice.

BUILDING THE FIRE

In order to light your fire, good conditions must be created for the flames. If you ask a firefighter how a fire is started and catches, they will probably begin by telling you about the fire triangle, which is one of the cornerstones of their job. The fire triangle is made up of the elements oxygen, heat, and a combustible material—if you remove one of these elements, the fire goes out. Having this in the back of your mind will make it easier to troubleshoot if you're having trouble getting the fire to burn.

Oxygen

A campfire requires oxygen (O_2), which converts carbon (C) to carbon dioxide (CO_2). So if your firewood is dry and you still find it difficult to get the fire started, or if it is overly smoky, it is probably because there is not enough oxygen present. In this case, it often helps to loosen the firewood up a little so it lies less compactly, or blow air on the embers so the fire can "breathe."

Combustible material

It is obvious that a campfire requires combustible material, but that material must also be dry. If you have ever tried to light a fire using wet firewood, then you'll know how important this is—you'd need supernatural powers to start a fire with wet wood. Once the fire has started up, adding a couple of damper logs can work. But when first lighting it up, it is essential that your firewood is dry.

Heat

Heat is a relative term. How high the temperature should be is determined by the different ignition points of different types of wood. You can blow all you want on the embers, but if they are not warm enough, you will not reach the ignition point. In this case, the only thing to do is to take a look at your ignition.

IGNITION

Ignition takes place in three stages. First with ignition material, then small sticks, and finally logs of firewood. Do not use lighter fluids or oils—first, because this contaminates the food and its flavor, and second, because it takes away some of the joy of making the fire. Make sure you have prepared and have everything you need at hand before you begin. Then you will avoid having to run around or stress over where to find more combustible material while you should be focusing on keeping the fire going.

Tinder

Good materials for getting the fire started include bark, small, dry sticks, or dry leaves. Light the tinder with a fire steel. The most important thing here is that you use something that catches fast and that there is plenty of it.

I usually peel off some of the outer parts of the bark of my firewood and tear these into strips until I have a good handful to light up with.

Kindling

Kindling is comprised of small pieces of wood (about the size of a pencil), preferably frayed and cracked, with as many surfaces as possible where the fire can catch. These small sticks are used to create the heart of the campfire. I either split a piece of firewood into smaller pieces or gather dry twigs from nature. Your kindling acts as a medium between the tinder and the firewood. The tinder does not create enough heat to make the firewood burn, but it causes the kindling to burn warmly enough and for long enough to ignite your firewood. Once you have your tinder lit, put the sticks on to form what looks like a small campfire. A good handful should be plenty. Once the tinder has caused the kindling to catch fire, the rest of the fire is built up around the kindling (the heart of the fire). Depending on which campfire you want to build, this is done either continuously or before lighting up.

Tinder

Kindling

FIREWOOD

All types of firewood produce the same amount of heat per kilogram of dry matter, but they do not all weigh the same. Lighter types of wood are highly flammable and easy to split, but they burn out quickly. The drier the matter, the higher the heating value. Beech, oak, ash, and birch have a higher heating value than, for example, willow, pine, and spruce, and are therefore more suitable for your campfire. Personally, I usually go with birch, even though other types such as beech have a higher heating value. Birch is easy to light up because it contains a flammable wood tar that ignites quickly. Furthermore, it is often relatively cheap to buy and is easy for me to find where I live. So for me, it is not always the heating value that determines the type of wood I use. The most important thing is that it must be dry. I'd also strongly recommend that you avoid firewood that contains high amounts of resin because it makes the food bitter and unpalatable.

How do I know if my firewood is dry?
Wood consists of small tubes that carry water up to the crown, so even long after the tree is cut down and split, water can remain inside. If your firewood is not dry enough, the heat energy must first be used to dry out the wood before it can ignite. If your firewood feels heavy and blunt when you hit two pieces against each other, it is not dry enough. Dry wood will sound almost hollow. Look for firewood that comes apart from the bark easily; wood uses water to adhere to the bark. Also pay attention to the color: if the split wood is dark and gray in color, it is typically drier than firewood that looks bright and fresh.

Types of firewood
Beech: High heating value, moderately easy to split
Oak: High heating value, easy to split
Ash: High heating value, easy to split
Birch: Medium-high heating value, moderately easy to split
Maple: Medium-high heating value, moderately easy to split
Pine: Low heating value, easy to split
Spruce: Low heating value, very easy to split

Size matters
The campfires in this book are made with birchwood measuring about 12–14 × 3–4 inches (30–35 × 8–10 cm) and weighing about 55 ounces (1,500 grams). In my experience, this size of firewood provides the most structured campfire with an optimum burn rate, embers of a good size, and an appropriate level of smoke production. But of course, there are exceptions that are handy to know about.

Smaller pieces of firewood
If you split the firewood into smaller pieces, it will gain a larger surface area and the fire will burn faster. The smoke will disappear faster, which is nice to have in mind if, for example, there are children around the fire. Kids will often be scared away from the fire if they get smoke in their eyes. The embers will be smaller and very intense, but will last only for a short while. This isn't always a disadvantage. For example, it will be absolutely perfect for the oyster recipe in this book. However, it is impractical if your food needs to cook for a long time.

Larger pieces of firewood
If, on the other hand, you choose to work with very large pieces of firewood, you will find that there will be more smoke over a longer period of time, the fire will burn more slowly, and the embers will last longer. This is perfect if you want to work a lot of smoky flavor into raw ingredients that will be cooked over a long period of time. But you must be aware that it may also be harder to control this type of campfire. In some places the fire will burn intensely while others remain untouched by the flames, so your campfire will burn unevenly. With a barge pole and some dexterity, you can restructure it and regain control, but ultimately you'll have an easier time with more moderately sized firewood.

EIGHT TYPES OF CAMPFIRES

LOG CABIN FIRE

This is an easy-to-make and highly flammable campfire that develops a good level of upward heat and produces large embers. The structure of the fire means that it is well ventilated and the firewood constantly feeds the flames, so it requires minimal maintenance. Depending on how closely you pack the firewood, it will light up faster or more slowly. If you pack the wood loosely, you'll get a quick ignition but also a faster burnout. The log cabin fire is a very useful, standard campfire (and my personal favorite) that provides a reliable ignition. It is a campfire that, once lit, will take care of itself without too much maintenance while the food is prepared. The vast majority of recipes in this book are made on a log cabin fire.

How to make it: Place three pieces of firewood in your firepit. Place the tinder between the pieces of wood and ignite. Add the kindling and start building the fire, first by laying three pieces of firewood across the three at the bottom. Then add a couple more layers, each perpendicular to the previous layer, alternating so that each new layer stacks over the one beneath.

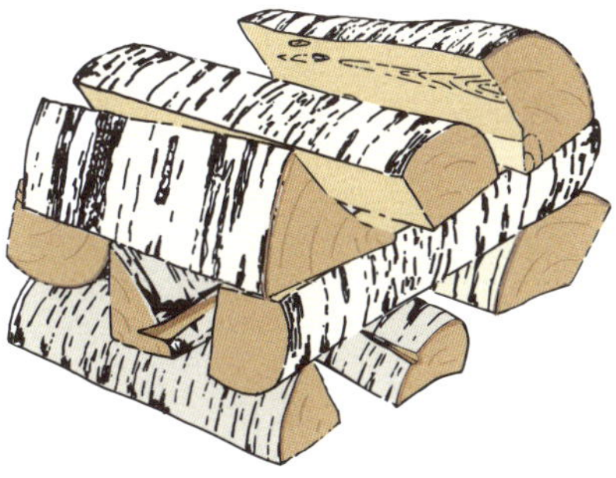

RAKOVALKEA FIRE

The *rakovalkea* fire is an ancient Viking campfire that burns for a very long time. In the old days, a large trunk would be split and ignited, but that's just overkill in my opinion, so this is my adaptation. The *rakovalkea* fire is great for long-term cooking techniques that require the use of radiant heat, such as *asado* or rotisserie.

How to make it: Stack two or more pieces of firewood on top of each other like a sandwich and hammer some branch pieces into the ground so that they stand vertically and hold the firewood in place. Place the tinder and kindling on a piece of bark so that you can move these under the firewood once they have ignited. Light the tinder, place it between the pieces of firewood, and feed it with the kindling. The fire may be a little difficult to make catch at first, as ventilation is not always optimal. But be patient, and use a fan or blow on it, and once it ignites, you'll be rewarded with an impressive fire that burns for a very long time.

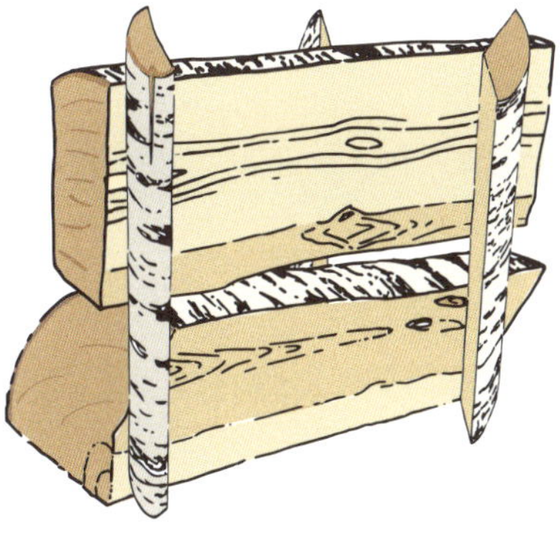

TEEPEE FIRE

This quickly made campfire is great for cooking something rapidly. It will not burn for a long time without maintenance, so it is best suited for short cooking times. Without maintenance, the structure of the pyramid does not last long before it collapses and becomes messy. To be frank, a teepee fire is probably best used as a casual campfire and heat source if you just plan to sit around it grilling marshmallows rather than doing any "real" cooking.

How to make it: Lay the tinder directly on the ground and build a small teepee shape around it with kindling (make a small opening for the ignition). Build a larger teepee around the small one, and ignite.

STAR CAMPFIRE

This campfire resembles those you often see in Western movies: a large bonfire that requires some space and burns for a long time at relatively low heat. In other words, it is great for slow cooking. The fire requires constant maintenance and is therefore best suited for situations where you plan to stay around the fire.

How to make it: Start by making a teepee fire following the instructions above. Around the teepee, lay three to five large, long pieces of firewood in a star-shaped formation. As the fire burns, feed it by pushing the ends of the stems inward.

HUNTER'S FIRE

This very nice and stable campfire burns for a long time. It is a great fire for cooking, as you can put equipment such as a pan or grill rack on the larger piece of firewood.

How to make it: Place two large pieces of firewood parallel to each other. Build a smaller log cabin or teepee shape between the two and ignite. The best results are achieved by placing the firewood in the same direction as the wind is blowing so that the wood doesn't block air from getting into the fire.

SWEDISH TORCH

Back in the day, woodworkers used this fire to heat their coffee, and it's really effective if you need to put your pots, kettles, or pans on the fire.

However, it is less practical if you're going to be working with the embers. Still, it looks festive, and also works well as a "supplement" fire next to a bigger campfire.

How to make it: A Swedish torch can be made in two ways. One requires a chainsaw, the other an axe. With the chainsaw, make two to three cuts in a reasonably thick log about two-thirds of the way down. Fill the cuts in the log with kindling and tinder and ignite. For the axe method, the log is split into four to six pieces. The pieces are then hammered into the ground until one-third of their length is buried. They should be close together but with a small space between them. Fill the space with kindling and tinder and ignite.

LEAN-TO FIRE

If conditions are especially windy, it can be challenging to light a fire. A lean-to fire provides the necessary shelter while also ensuring there's enough ventilation for ignition. This is a campfire that burns rapidly, so you'll be able to get cooking with it quickly. Along with the log cabin fire, this is one of my personal favorites.

How to make it: First, position a large piece of firewood so that it shields your fire from whichever direction the wind is blowing. Place your tinder close to the firewood, then place your kindling so that it is leaning against the large piece of firewood. Finally, put your remaining firewood on top of everything else. There should be some space between the pieces of firewood, but not too much, as the fire will be well ventilated from below.

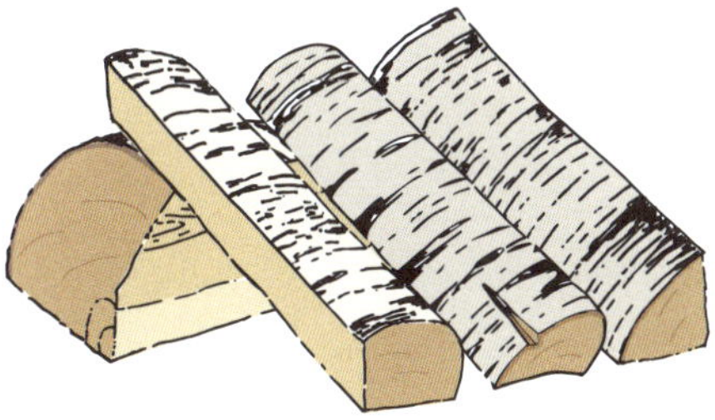

KEYHOLE FIRE

A keyhole fire is great if you're going to be working with your fire for a long time. It requires a lot of space but provides much greater temperature control in return, plus the opportunity to make several different dishes at the same time.

How to make it: Build a log cabin, teepee, or lean-to fire. Connect two pieces of firewood to the main fire as if you were going to make a hunter's fire. Ignite your campfire (the "mother fire") and feed it regularly, so that it is constantly up and running. Continuously shovel the embers from the main fire into the space between the two pieces of wood ("the hearth"), so you always have fresh embers without flames.

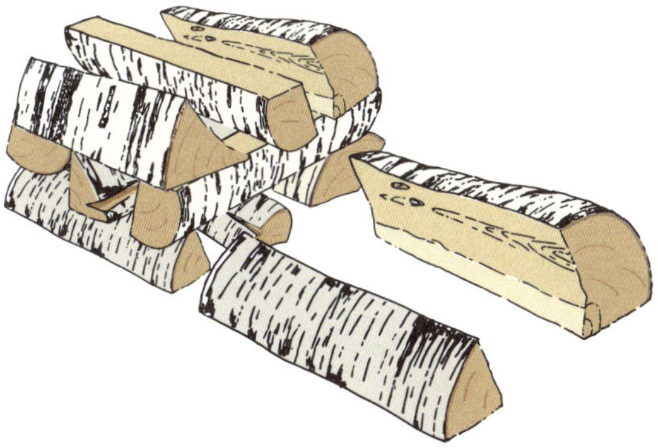

LIGHT YOUR FIRE

HOW TO LIGHT A FIRE

1. Decide what kind of fire you want to build
2. Decide where to build the fire
3. Prepare the tinder
4. Prepare the kindling
5. Prepare the firewood
6. Make a small nest of the tinder and light it up
7. Once the tinder is burning well, add the kindling
8. Build your fire around the flames

THE NINE LIVES OF A CAMPFIRE

The campfire has nine lives, from ignition to burnout, and each of these phases has different characteristics and temperatures. Knowing and understanding the different phases and what to use them for makes it much easier to cook with fire, and to achieve great results. Once familiar with the nine phases, you'll have a better understanding of the process and a better feeling for when to start your cooking, and—more importantly—when not to start chucking your food into the flames. Every recipe comes with a campfire strength recommendation to use as a guideline for how hot your campfire should be before you begin your food preparation.

1–2: Start-up
These stages are primarily about getting the fire lit up before you start cooking. Fires burn unevenly at these two stages with relatively low temperatures and unstable smoke generation, which means they are rarely useful for fully cooking anything.

3–4: Flames and smoke (Indirect heat)
These stages provide the most stable smoke generation, and also the biggest flames. You must therefore be careful when placing food directly over flames at these stages, as it may become sooty in appearance. You'll usually use this campfire strength for dishes that need to be cooked with indirect heat.

5–6: Intense embers (Direct heat)
Here the flames begin to settle, intense embers are created, and the smoke generation becomes weaker but more stable. This is the ideal time to grill, either directly in the embers or on a grill rack placed above them. If you add a new piece of firewood or fresh leaves or wood at this point, you'll get the best of both worlds. The hot embers create a good, solid Maillard reaction, and the fresh wood adds a smoky flavor to the food.

7–9: Calm embers (Isolated heat)
This phase is the campfire equivalent of turning the stove down slightly, with stable embers that are perfect for food that needs to be cooked for a little while.

1. *Ignition* (200–400°F/100–200°C)
2. *Lighting* (400–570°F/200–300°C)
3. *Burn-up* (570–1,100°F/300–600°C)
4. *Burnout* (1,100–1,800°F/600–1,000°C)
5. *Intense embers* (1,800–2,200°F/1,000–1,200°C+)
6. *Embers* (2,000–1,650°F/1,100–900°C)
7. *Hot embers* (1,650–1,300°F/900–700°C)
8. *Warm embers* (1,300–950°F/700–500°C)
9. *Afterheat* (950–32°F/500–0°C)

1
2
3
4
5
6
7
8
9

TYPES OF HEAT AND COOKING METHODS

Before building your campfire, give some thought to the estimated cooking time and the cooking techniques you are going to use. They are of great importance when deciding what kind of heat source will be most appropriate. Usually, the solution is rather obvious. First and foremost, it is important to notice that when cooking with fire, you rarely cook directly over the flames. This will coat your food in soot and make it look dirty or even burn it. Instead, use either the indirect heat emitted by the flames, the direct heat from the embers, or the insulated heat from ashes, embers, or stones.

INDIRECT HEAT

This method is great, especially for cuts of meat that need to cook for longer periods of time—those that taste best with a nice, smoky taste and a gentler treatment of the ingredients. Here you'll want to keep your food a little distance away from the fire. Cooking with indirect heat typically takes a good amount of time, and you need to keep a close eye on the temperature of your fire and the location of your ingredients during the preparation. You cannot just leave the food to cook on the fire and then go off to do something else. This is also important because the fire must be maintained so that the flames are consistent.

CLINCHING

Clinching involves simply putting your food directly on the embers to cook. This exposes the food to an intense, direct heat, which is suitable for coloring and caramelizing. It is great to use for meat that needs to be quickly browned before further cooking. It's also suitable for vegetables that have a "sacrificial layer," that is, an outer layer. It can be quite daunting the first time you do it, and you'll probably feel as though the food will burn up quickly and become tainted by the ashes. But fear not: you'll actually be putting the food on the embers rather than the ashes, and you'll be surprised at how clean it actually is when you pick it up. Furthermore, it will probably surprise you just how long your food takes to cook this way. It doesn't happen as fast as you'd expect. Avoid oil or butter when you put ingredients directly into the embers, as it may catch on fire—you're not interested in creating flames with this technique.

COOKING OVER EMBERS

This is another direct heat method, but one that offers a higher degree of control than clinching. Using this technique, you can move your food further away from or closer to the hot embers, depending on the kind of heat you want. You'll need something to support the produce with, a grill rack, string, skewer, or the like. Your chosen tool should be placed at an appropriate height over the embers (make sure there are no flames). The food should be hanging or lying "naked," without any kind of covering. Make sure that it is possible to turn the food around as you cook it.

INSULATED HEAT

Using this method, you're able to shield the food from direct contact with the heat. You do this by wrapping the food up, utilizing its own natural peel, covering it, digging it into the ground, or whatever else you can think of. This is a gentle way of cooking that heats up the juices in your ingredients and practically steams the food from the inside.

PRACTICALITIES AND SAFETY

Build your own firepit
If you have the opportunity, I would recommend that you build your own firepit near your home. This makes it easier to make the campfire a regular part of your life, plus it's handy to have a fixed place where you can cook. Of course, you can use a metal brazier, but you won't have quite the same types of options as you would with an old-fashioned firepit.

Find the right place
Place the firepit so that it is sheltered from the wind, with plenty of working space around it. Make sure you are at a reasonable distance from trees, shrubs, and other combustible material. Think about your surroundings in relation to the smoke. If the place you have chosen for your firepit is right next to your neighbor's bedroom window, you may need to rethink your location.

Prepare the foundations
In your kitchen, you want your food to be level while cooking so the sauce doesn't slip down to one end of the pot. The same applies to your firepit. So get the surface roughly level either by digging out or adding in soil. The bottom of the firepit should, of course, be nonflammable. Lay gravel, sand, or rocks at the bottom so you are sure that the fire cannot spread. Also, keep in mind that during the dry months there may be a risk of causing a ground ignition that can spread very quickly via tree roots. Therefore, make sure you apply a generous layer of nonflammable material.

Frame the fireplace
Use either large stones or stems to frame the firepit so that the embers do not spread and so the radiant heat is shielded. Make sure to keep a good distance between the fire and the frame so that you have a place for skewers, rotisserie, grill grates, and other tools.

Safety and common sense
Part of the joy of campfire cooking is working with the fire, which has its own life. But that is exactly why you need to give security some extra thought before you start. Open fire is something that can make people around you feel anxious, so don't be blasé about it. Do yourself the favor of being the one who always acts professionally around the fire. That is the best way of dealing with potential naysayers.

Tell the neighbors what you are doing
Unfortunately, lighting a fire is not seen as such a normal thing to do these days, so it can make people apprehensive when it is suddenly smoking away in their backyard. So let your neighbors know what you are doing—it could

be an excellent opportunity to invite them over for a beer by the fire. Or, at the very least, it will prevent the firefighters from showing up at your door during your campfire session when someone decides to call the emergency services.

Leave the lighter fluid and lamp oil in the tool shed
You won't need them. In the worst-case scenario, you run the risk of injuries and damage caused by flames running wild. In the best-case scenario, your food will taste bad.

Never use painted or impregnated wood for your fire
Although it's tempting to get rid of some old wood and save a trip to the recycling station, painted or impregnated wood develops a lot of polluting smoke, which is good for neither the environment nor your food—and you don't want to risk having the local fire department over for dinner.

Keep water within close reach
If an accident should occur, it is important to act quickly and prevent the fire from spreading.

Use a brazier, or better yet, make a firepit
If you build a fire in the yard, do so at a safe distance from the house and surrounding fences, trees, and shrubs. Be sure not to build the fire on a flammable surface. Pebbles, gravel, and sand are all suitable as foundations for your campfire.

If you build a campfire in nature, make sure to comply with local guidelines
Always check local rules and regulations before heading out.

Do not leave a lit fire
And always extinguish it with water, especially if you are at the beach. I strongly advise that you do not cover it with sand or dig the fire down, as the sand can retain the heat for hours after you have left.

Those were the words, now let's cook!

VEGETABLES

SMOKED BABY BROCCOLI

WITH SOUR CREAM & CASHEWS

Log cabin, lean-to, or hunter's fire

5–6

Coarse-mesh sieve

SERVES 2–4

- 10–12 baby broccoli
- salt
- olive oil
- 1 handful of fresh dill
- 1 handful of salted and roasted cashews
- ½ cup (100 ml) sour cream, 38% fat

Start by lighting your fire and let it burn to fire strength 5. Put a few pieces of fresh firewood on the fire so it starts to develop smoke.

Remove dirt and any brown parts from the baby broccoli. Rinse them and place in a coarse-mesh sieve. Sprinkle with salt and olive oil.

Keep the sieve directly over the smoking embers. Let the baby broccoli cook for about 5 minutes, turning frequently by shaking the sieve. You want the outer florets to scorch a bit here and there.

Arrange on a plate with dill, nuts, and sour cream, and sprinkle with a few generous drops of olive oil.

BUTTERNUT SQUASH

WITH EGG & CHILI

Log cabin, lean-to, or hunter's fire

6–7

SERVES 4

- 1 butternut squash
- 2 eggs
- olive oil
- salt
- 10 pickled chilies (see p. 255)

Start by lighting your fire and allow the embers to burn out a little before setting your squash on them.

Cut the butternut squash into halves and place the 2 halves (cut-side down) directly on the embers. Grill until they get some color to them—about 7–10 minutes. Turn the squash over and scrape out the kernels with a spoon. Crack an egg into each space where the kernels were and pour a few drops of olive oil over. Sprinkle with salt and allow the squash to bake in the embers until it is tender and the eggs have set—about 20–30 minutes.

Take the butternut squash out of the embers. Slice the pickled chilies and place them on top of the squash.

WHITE ONIONS

WITH SUGAR-SALTED EGG YOLKS

Log cabin, lean-to, or hunter's fire

7–8

SERVES 3

- 1 cup (250 g) coarse salt
- 1 ¼ cup (250 g) sugar
- 15 bay leaves
- 9 egg yolks
- 1 cup (200 ml) apple juice
- 2 tbsp. apple vinegar (see p. 249)
- 1 tbsp. good olive oil
- 2 white onions

Blend together salt, sugar, and bay leaves. Sprinkle half of the sugar/salt mixture into the bottom of a dish and make 9 spherical indentations in the mixture with the back of a spoon. Carefully place an egg yolk into each identation and cover with the rest of the sugar/salt. Let the yolks stand like this for 5–6 hours.

Light the fire and let it burn to calm embers.

Boil the apple juice into a syrup with half of the vinegar. Add a little more vinegar if needed: you want the taste to be very sweet and sour. Stir in the olive oil.

Put the white onions with the peel directly on the embers until the surface is completely burned and the onions appear tender when you press on them. Cut the onions from bottom to top and separate each layer, starting from the middle. Take 9 nice slices and place on a plate with the curved part facing down so that they each create a small bowl. Drizzle a spoonful of the syrup into each.

Scrape the salt off the top of the egg yolks and gently lift them up. Lightly rinse them with water, place an egg yolk into each onion bowl, and serve.

PARSNIP "ROADKILL"

WITH BROWNED BUTTER & PAPRIKA

Log cabin, lean-to, or hunter's fire

5–8

Campfire pan

SERVES 2–4

- 2 large parsnips, at least 5 ½ oz. (150 g) each
- 8 ¾ oz. (250 g) butter
- 4 dried figs
- 2 egg yolks
- 2 tbsp. white wine vinegar
- salt
- olive oil
- 1 tbsp. smoked paprika

Start by lighting the fire and let it burn to embers.

Wash the parsnips, wrap them in aluminum foil, and place them directly on the embers. Cook the parsnips for 1–1 ½ hours or until they are very tender.

Meanwhile, make the sauce: Over the embers where the parsnips are cooking, place the campfire pan and let it heat up. Put the butter in a saucepan and place it on the campfire pan. Allow the butter to sizzle and become brown in the saucepan. Let it get plenty of color so that the butter itself is brown and not just the whey. There is a golden moment when the whey turns almost black and the butter browns, which is magical and just what we're aiming for. Strain the whey off. Take a bit of the browned butter and put the dried figs in it. Put the egg yolks in a saucepan and add the white wine vinegar and some salt. Whisk over the heat from the fire until the egg yolks are thick and creamy. Remove the saucepan from the heat and add the rest of the browned butter a little at a time while constantly whipping. When all the butter is absorbed, add salt and vinegar to taste.

Now unpack the parsnips and gently remove the peel with a knife. Place the parsnips one by one between 2 pieces of baking paper and press flat until about ½-inch (1-cm) thick. Sprinkle olive oil on both sides and fry the parsnips until golden on the campfire pan.

Arrange the parsnips with the warm figs and the sauce. Use a sieve to sprinkle over the smoked paprika, and serve.

ENDIVE

WITH CARAMELIZED BLOOD ORANGE

Rakovalkea fire

3–4

Rotisserie (or a debarked stick and 2 Y-shaped sticks), grill net, brush

SERVES 4

- 3 blood oranges
- ½ cup (100 ml) good liquid honey
- 2 endives
- fine salt
- olive oil

Start by lighting the fire and let it burn until it has nice, even flames. You want to have a radiant heat as even as possible so that the caramelization of the blood oranges is evenly distributed.

Peel each orange as follows: Cut the top and bottom off with a sharp knife. Then let the knife run from top to bottom while following the shape of the orange. Put the oranges on your rotisserie skewer and allow them to fry as they rotate continuously. When they start to feel warm on the surface, brush with honey and sprinkle with a little fine salt. Repeat this process at least 3 times while the blood oranges are roasting. They should cook for about 30 minutes, depending on the size of the oranges and the temperature of the fire.

Split the endives and place in your grill net. Sprinkle with a little fine salt and olive oil.

Carefully remove the blood oranges from the skewer and overturn the fire so that the embers are exposed. Place the grill net with the endives on the embers and grill on both sides until they are nicely colored and appear tender and juicy.

Take the endives out of the net and sprinkle with salt and olive oil. Place on a dish with the blood oranges, and serve.

"As a chef's apprentice at the French restaurant Le Sommelier in Copenhagen, I was first introduced to the combination of blood orange and endive. At the time, I didn't understand what it was all about. I had a hard time getting past the bitterness to the sweetness that unites the two. It's like with coffee, blue cheese, and beer, where the taste can be overwhelming the first time you try it. The taste for endive is one that needs to be learned. The good thing is that those kinds of tastes are often the ones you end up loving the most."

—Nicolai

BURNT LEEKS

WITH GOAT CHEESE

Log cabin, lean-to, or teepee fire

2–4

SERVES 3–4

- 2–3 large, thick leeks
- 3 ½ oz. (100 g) of a good, semi-soft goat cheese
- olive oil
- salt and pepper

Light a fire and let it burn to large flames.

Put the leeks directly in the flames and burn them until they are completely black. It is important to have a sacrificial layer, so you don't have to spend time peeling them first.

When the leeks are black all over, press on them lightly to feel if they are soft inside. If not, put them back in the fire. Depending on the size, they should cook for between 10 and 15 minutes.

Remove the leeks from the fire and gently pull off the outer, burnt layers so that the light green and tender parts appear.

Cut the leeks into halves and spread them out slightly on a plate, toss chunks of the goat cheese over them, and add a little olive oil, salt, and pepper to taste.

"While working on this book, Nicolai often shared the dishes with our neighbors. He'd go over with a plate every now and then, get their feedback, and have a chat about the weather. But unfortunately, they never had the chance to try this dish—it tasted so good that I ate it all before it got that far. Sorry, neighbors!"

—Eva

MÅNDAG 05 MARS 2018
hotellrum
Notiser

BURNT SAVOY CABBAGE

WITH VINAIGRETTE

Log cabin, lean-to, or hunter's fire

4–5

SERVES 4

- 1 savoy cabbage
- 2 eggs
- 3 tbsp. capers
- 1 cup parsley
- 1 cup chervil
- 2 banana shallots
- 1 tbsp. Dijon mustard
- 2 cups (500 ml) sherry vinegar
- ½ cup (100 ml) olive oil
- salt

Light the fire and let it burn up to large flames.

Place the savoy cabbage directly in the flames. Let it burn for about 20–30 minutes, depending on size. Check the temperature inside the cabbage along the way by poking a pointed knife into the center, letting the knife sit for a few seconds, then pulling it out quickly and gently touching the knife to your lower lip to feel how warm it is. The cabbage is ready when the knife feels very hot.

Wet a few pages of newspaper and wrap the whole eggs separately. Place the eggs directly in the hot embers for 10 minutes.

Meanwhile, make the vinaigrette. Finely chop capers, parsley, chervil, and shallots. Mix with mustard, vinegar, and oil, and season with salt.

Take the cabbage out of the flames and remove the outer, burnt leaves. Cut it into 8 wedges. Put the cabbage into a bowl and pour the vinaigrette over it. Take the eggs out of the embers and remove the shells. Tear or cut them into smaller pieces over the cabbage.

BLACK CABBAGE

"DOLMAS"

Log cabin, lean-to, or hunter's fire

7–8

Butcher's twine

SERVES 2–4

- 6 black cabbage leaves
- 1 tbsp. coarse mustard
- 4 slices of pancetta
- 2 really good mozzarella cheeses
- 1 banana shallot
- 2 cloves of garlic
- ¼ cup (60 ml) good olive oil
- juice of 1 lemon
- salt and pepper

Light the fire and let it burn to embers.

Wash the black cabbage leaves and place them on the table so that the leaves overlap longitudinally. Start by making the first "dolma." Smear the cabbage with half of the mustard and place 2 slices of pancetta on top of the leaves. Tear mozzarella cheese into small pieces over the pancetta. Cut the shallot into fine rings and toss a small handful over the cheese. Grate the garlic and stir it together with olive oil and lemon juice. Pour plenty of the marinade over the leaves. Season with salt and pepper.

Roll a black cabbage leaf to make what looks like a torpedo. Lace the roll with butcher's twine. Repeat with each leaf. Just before cooking, pour water over the rolls. This will prevent the leaves from burning before the mozzarella is hot. Place the rolls directly onto the embers and turn, rotating them constantly. The cabbage may very well gain some color but should not burn (though burning a corner or two is nothing to worry about). After a few minutes, the rolls will give in when you press on them lightly and appear warm all the way through. Take them out of the embers.

Remove the string and slice the rolls open from top to bottom. Put them on a plate, and pour a little more of the marinade over if you have some left.

BURNT BEET

WITH PICKLED ELDERFLOWERS

Log cabin, lean-to, or teepee fire

5–6

SERVES 4

- ¼ cup (25 g) light mustard seeds
- 1 cup (235 ml) apple vinegar (see p. 249)
- 1 large beet, at least 2 ¼ lbs. (1 kg), preferably heavier
- salt
- 5–10 pickled elderflowers (see p. 253)

This is a real winter dish that should be served steaming hot. If you've had a little foresight and pickled some of the summer's fine flowers while they blossomed, it can also be a dish that evokes nostalgic memories of brighter days. Pickled rosehip petals (see p. 251) work just as well as elderflowers, and if you don't have any flowers at all, just add a dash of a good, aromatic vinegar.

Start the day before by pickling the mustard seeds. Simply pour the seeds into a glass, pour the apple vinegar over, stir, and leave them—the longer the better.

Light the fire and let it burn to strength 5.

Put the beet directly into the embers and cover with a few large embers. Let it turn completely black. The outside will be cut off, so you don't have to bother washing or peeling the beet. It should cook like this for at least 1 hour, and probably longer—how long depends on the shape and size of the beet. Test if it is ready by sticking a knife into it and seeing if it feels completely tender inside, because then it is probably done. However, remember that it is better to overcook it rather than undercook it.

Take the burnt beet out of the embers and cut off all that is black. Cut it into coarse pieces and season with salt. Arrange the dish with pickled elderflowers and small blobs of the pickled mustard seeds.

SALT-BAKED QUINCES

WITH BROWNED BUTTER & BUCKWHEAT

Log cabin, lean-to, or hunter's fire

5–9

Dutch oven, campfire stand, grill rack

SERVES 4

- 2 quinces
- 2 ¼ – 4 ½ lbs. (1 – 2 kg) salt
- 1 cup (200 g) butter
- 1 oz. (30 g) buckwheat kernels
- 1 oz. (30 g) Parmesan cheese
- 1 handful of chickweed (a very common weed—you can most likely find it somewhere in your surroundings)

Light the fire and let it burn to embers.

Cover the bottom of your Dutch oven with a layer of coarse salt ¾-inch (2-cm) thick. Place the quinces whole in the salt (make sure they do not touch each other) and cover them with the remaining salt. Put the lid on the pot and hang it over the fire. Put some embers on the lid of the Dutch oven and let the quinces bake in the salt for 1 ½ hours. Make sure to feed the campfire along the way if needed.

Meanwhile, make the browned butter. Put the butter in a saucepan and place it in the embers. Let the butter sizzle so that the whey starts to fry. When you can see that the whey is dark and the clear part of the butter has changed color from yellow to light brown, take it off the heat. Strain the butter to remove the whey. Add the buckwheat kernels. Put the saucepan back into the embers and let the kernels roast in the butter. When the buckwheat kernels are golden and crisp, pour the butter and kernels into a bowl.

Now take out the quinces. Take your Dutch oven off the fire and remove the lid. Gently hit the hard salt shell with the back of a spoon until the quinces appear. Lift them up and peel them gently by letting a knife catch a little peel, and tear (like when you peel new potatoes).

Cut the quinces into wedges, place a grill rack over the fire, and grill the quinces until they are colored on both sides. Serve them on a plate with the buckwheat kernels, the warm browned butter, and Parmesan cheese, in chunks or grated. Decorate with a handful of chickweed, and serve.

GRILLED OYSTER MUSHROOMS

WITH GARLIC & THYME

Log cabin or teepee fire

3–4

Grill net

SERVES 4

- 7 oz. (200 g) oyster mushrooms
- ½ cup (100 g) butter
- 3 cloves of garlic, grated
- 10 twigs of thyme
- salt

Light the fire and let it burn to embers.

Place the oyster mushrooms in a grill net and push its handle into the ground or place the grill net firmly with some large stones holding it down. The aim is to expose the mushrooms to radiant heat only.

Melt the butter, and add the grated garlic and the leaves of the thyme.

Spread the butter with a spoon or brush all over the mushrooms as you grill them. Turn the grill net and repeat on the other side.

Season with salt, and serve.

GREEN ASPARAGUS SANDWICH

Log cabin, lean-to, or hunter's fire

5–6

Grill rack

SERVES 4

- 32 thin green asparagus spears
- olive oil
- salt
- juice and zest of 1 lemon
- 4 flatbreads (see p. 231)
- ¾ cup (200 ml) Greek yogurt
- 5 ½ oz. (150 g) semi-hard, flavorful cheese (I used Västerbotten cheese)
- 1 large handful of fresh herbs, such as broadleaf parsley, coriander, and tarragon

Light the fire and let it burn to embers. Clean and then crack or cut the bottom from the green asparagus.

Grill the asparagus for about 2 minutes on each side. Put them in a bowl and season with olive oil, salt, lemon juice, and zest, and turn well. Put 8 asparagus spears and a good dollop of yogurt onto each flatbread. Grate or break the cheese over the asparagus. Coarsely chop the herbs and sprinkle over generously.

Fold the bread, and serve.

ASPARAGUS

WITH BEECH LEAVES

Log cabin, teepee, or lean-to fire

7–8

SERVES 2

- 15 large green and white asparagus spears
- ½ cup (100 ml) smoked butter (see p. 257)
- 2 tbsp. elderflower vinegar (see p. 253)
- 1 handful of newly sprouted beech leaves
- salt

Light the fire and let it burn to calm embers.

Put the asparagus directly into the embers and let them turn black, cooking 3–5 minutes.

Meanwhile, melt the butter in a saucepan and add vinegar to taste.

Remove the asparagus from the embers and peel the spears while they are still warm from top to bottom with a potato peeler. Cut ¾–1 ¼ inch (2–3 cm) off the bottoms to remove the thready part.

Sprinkle with salt and arrange the asparagus on a platter with the beech leaves and butter vinaigrette.

ARTICHOKES

WITH GARLIC & PARSLEY

Log cabin, lean-to, or hunter's fire

5–6

Grill rack

SERVES 2–4

- 8 artichokes
- 1 bundle of broadleaf parsley
- 4 lemons
- 3 cloves of garlic
- ½ cup (100 ml) olive oil

Light the fire.

Then start preparing the artichokes. Fill a large pot with plenty of cold water, preferably 4–5 quarts (4–5 liters). Take half of the parsley, tear it into rough pieces, and place in the water. Cut 2 lemons into halves and squeeze the juice into the water. The parsley and lemon prevent the artichokes from turning brown.

Prepare each artichoke for cooking as follows: Touch the artichoke head and find the place where the meat feels firm. Make a cut directly over it so that you cut the top off the flower and expose the heart. Immediately dip the artichoke into the water and take it out again. The rule of thumb is that every time you make an incision, it must be dipped. Let the knife follow the heart around so you cut off the leaves and reach the center, and dip the artichoke into the water again. Finally, peel the stem by letting the knife follow the stem down to the head, and remove the remaining leaves. Again, dip in water. In the center of the heart are some soft hairs that are unpleasant to eat. Use either a spoon or the knife to remove them. Cut the hearts into halves and place them in the water. Repeat until all artichoke hearts are in the water. Pour 2 handfuls of salt into the water and place the pot in the embers, cover with a lid, and bring to a boil.

Meanwhile, prepare the garlic oil: finely chop or grate the garlic cloves and mix with the olive oil.

When the water boils, transfer the artichokes to a bowl and pour the garlic oil over them.

Place a grill rack over the embers. Cut 2 lemons into halves and grill them until completely dark on the cut side. Grill the artichokes at the same time, until they have golden spots here and there and are tender when stuck with a knife. Sprinkle with salt and serve with the second half of parsley leaves and the grilled lemons.

HONEYDEW MELON

WITH PROSCIUTTO & ALMONDS

Log cabin or lean-to fire

5–6

Grill rack, coarse-mesh sieve

SERVES 4

- 1 honeydew melon
- ¾ cup (100 g) smoked almonds
- 1 cup (150 g) prosciutto ham, thinly sliced
- salt
- 3 tbsp. olive oil (use the good bottle of olive oil—the one you save for special occasions)

This is more of a concept than a recipe, with room for endless modifications. It also works with flavors like goat cheese, chorizo, capers, and black olives. In the photo, you may notice some chunks missing from the melon. This was not intentional. When I looked away for a moment, our youngest son grabbed the melon that I'd prepared and took a few juicy bites. But this actually turned out to be an advantage, because it made the surface of the melon uneven, giving it a nice caramelization. But if you don't have a six-year-old on hand, then I suggest that you break off a few pieces of the melon with a spoon instead.
—Nicolai

Light the fire and let it burn to the embers. Put the grill rack on the embers and let it get hot.

Cut the melon from top to bottom, scrape out the kernels, and carve a few cuts into the melon's meat with a spoon. Place the melon with the cut side on the grill rack and grill until it is amber in color and caramelized.

Take the melon off the grill rack and turn it upside-down. Place prosciutto ham and smoked almonds over the carved center, sprinkle with salt, drizzle well with olive oil, and serve with a spoon to dig out the filling.

CAULIFLOWER

AS KEBAB

Keyhole fire

7–8

1 skewer, about 3 feet (1 m), a blunt object to use for hammering it into the ground (e. g., the back of your axe), mortar and pestle

SERVES 4–6

- 1 star anise
- 3 cloves of garlic
- 1 cup (110 g) fresh coriander
- 1 clove
- 2 tsp. chili flakes
- 1 tbsp. ground cumin
- 1 small tuber of ginger, peeled
- 1 tbsp. smoked paprika
- 1 tbsp. salt, and more to taste
- 1 lemon, zest and juice (optional)
- 1 cup (200 g) Greek yogurt
- 1 cauliflower

You need a fire that burns solidly for this dish, and you cannot use a brazier, because the skewer must be hammered into the ground. Therefore, you need a good-sized space where you can build and light a nice, big campfire. When the fire is burning well, scrape some of the embers to one side and add more firewood. This way you always have fresh hot embers available.

Grind together all ingredients except the yogurt and cauliflower, using a mortar and pestle, until you have a homogeneous mixture. Pour the mixture into the yogurt and stir until the marinade is uniform. Add more salt and optional additional lemon juice to taste.

Cut the leaves off the cauliflower and keep as much of the stem as possible. Force the skewer straight through the cauliflower and rub with the marinade until the cauliflower is completely covered. There will be some marinade left over, to be used later. Beside the fire, push the spear into the ground so that it reaches about 8–12 inches (20–30 cm) above the embers.

Now it's time to give your cauliflower some love. Turn it every so often and add some extra embers along the way. Cook the cauliflower for about 1 hour, depending on the weather and outside temperature—keep an eye on the color and assume that the longer it cooks, the better it'll get. After ½ hour, lift the skewer, rotate it 180 degrees, and let the cooking process continue. Finally, pull the skewer up from the ground and smear the remaining marinade on the cauliflower. Grasp the end of the skewer and hold the cauliflower just above the embers, rotating it until the color is perfect. Then take the cauliflower off the skewer, divide into coarse pieces, and serve.

STAUB
STAUB

FENNEL
À LA BARIGOULE

Log cabin, lean-to, or hunter's fire

5–7

Grill rack, cast-iron campfire pan, pot with lid

SERVES 4

- 3 bulbs of fennel
- 2 onions
- 5 bay leaves
- 1 head of garlic
- 1 lemon, quartered
- 2–3 sprigs of thyme
- olive oil
- ½ cup (100 ml) apple vinegar (see p. 249)
- ¾ cup (200 ml) white wine
- 1 ¼ cup (300 ml) chicken stock

Light the fire and let it burn to embers. When it's ready, divide the fire into 2 parts so that you can put a grill rack over one side and your campfire pan over the other.

Split and grill the fennel bulbs until they are well colored.

Meanwhile, let the pot heat up on the fire. Split the onions and garlic and add to the pot along with bay leaves, the quartered lemon, and thyme. Add the olive oil to the pan and fry a little. Place the grilled fennel in the pan and add the apple vinegar. Stir and let cook until the vinegar has almost disappeared. Then add the white wine. Stir and cook until half of it has evaporated. Finally, add the chicken stock. Cover the pot with a lid and let it simmer for 40 minutes.

Lift the lid from the pot, and serve fennel immediately.

ONION SALAD

Log cabin, lean-to, or hunter's fire

5–6

Grill rack

SERVES 2

- 5 pearl onions
- 1 red onion
- 1 white onion
- 2 yellow onions, halved
- 3 tbsp. apple vinegar (see p. 249)
- 2 tbsp. olive oil
- salt
- 10 small ramson leaves

Light the fire and let it burn to embers.

Place the pearl onions, red onion, and white onion (with the peel on) directly onto the embers. The small onions should cook for about 5 minutes, the larger ones for about 10 minutes. Place a grill rack over the embers and grill the halved yellow onions until they are completely black on the cut side, and then turn them over. Continue grilling on the other side for about 5 minutes, until they feel tender when you give them a little squeeze. Take them off the grill rack and separate them into scales.

Remove the other onions from the embers. Carefully cut off the bottom of each onion and "slip" each onion as you would do with an almond. Cut the larger onions into halves and toss all the onions together with the vinegar, olive oil, and salt. Serve with the ransom leaves.

BURNT EGGPLANT

WITH CHERVIL BLANQUETTE

Log cabin, lean-to, or hunter's fire

7–8

SERVES 2

- 2 eggplants
- ⅔ cup (150 ml) dry sherry
- ⅔ cup (150 ml) dark veal stock
- 1 tbsp. white pepper
- ½ cup (115 g) butter
- 2 eggs
- 1 tbsp. crème fraîche, 38% fat
- 2 tbsp. (10 g) freshly grated ginger
- 1 tbsp. maple syrup
- 1 tsp. salt
- 1 bunch of chervil

Light the fire and let it burn to calm embers.

Place the eggplants directly into the fire for 20 minutes, turning them frequently. The peel acts as a fantastic insulator for the eggplant meat, so you don't have to worry about them burning.

Make the sauce by adding sherry, veal stock, white pepper, and butter to a saucepan, and stir. Bring to a boil, and reduce the sauce to about one-third of its original volume. Beat the eggs well, and add the crème fraîche, ginger, syrup, salt, and chervil (save a bit of chervil to use as garnish). Blend it all together and add the warm, reduced stock gradually while blending. Sift the sauce.

Make a cut in each eggplant and open it up a bit. Season the insides with salt and fill with the sauce. Sprinkle with the remaining chervil, and serve.

POTATO WAFER

WITH TOMATO CHUTNEY

Keyhole fire

6–8

Råd iron, coarse-mesh sieve, campfire stand, Dutch oven

MAKES 6 PIECES

- 1 red bell pepper
- 1 star anise
- 2 tbsp. sherry vinegar
- 1 tbsp. muscovado sugar
- 3 tomatoes
- 6 firm potatoes the size of golf balls
- olive oil
- salt
- 1 handful of chervil and cicely

I use my råd *iron (see equipment p. 13) for this recipe, but a waffle or Italian-style* pizzelle *iron will do as well—the thinner the better.*

Light the fire and let it burn to embers. Scrape the embers to one side. Place your campfire stand over the embers and hang your Dutch oven from it.

Put the bell pepper into the embers and let it cook until it is black all over. Pull off the black skin and split the pepper. Scrape the kernels out and discard along with the green stalk. Put the pepper in the Dutch oven with star anise, sherry vinegar, and muscovado sugar. Put a fresh piece of wood on the fire so that it produces more smoke.

Split the tomatoes and place them in a sieve with the cut side down. Place the sieve over the smoke for 10 minutes. Next, add the tomatoes to the other ingredients in your Dutch oven and let cook until all the liquid has evaporated. Add salt to taste.

Peel the potatoes and boil them in water with plenty of salt—use 1¾ (30 g) tbsp. per quart (or liter). The potatoes should be cooked a bit longer than if you were boiling potatoes to eat as they are, and slightly less than potatoes for mashing. Remove the potatoes from the water and let cool slightly.

Place the *råd* or waffle iron directly into the embers and heat it well for 5 minutes. Open the iron, add a tablespoon of oil, and distribute it well. Place potato on the lower surface, and press the iron together so that the potato is made completely flat. Some potato will be spilling out of the edges of the iron. Scrape this off with a knife. Put the iron back into the embers and flip it every minute. The potato should cook for about 5 minutes, or until golden and crispy. Repeat with the remaining boiled potatoes.

Serve the potato wafers with a bit of tomato chutney, chervil, and cicely leaves.

BURNT POTATOES

Log cabin, lean-to, or hunter's fire

6–7

SERVES 2

- 2 baking potatoes

Do not use aluminum foil for your baking potatoes—it will hold onto the water and the potatoes will eventually appear more cooked than baked. What you want is for them to dehydrate and absorb as much of the flavor from the campfire as possible. Instead of foil, I would suggest choosing large potatoes, because then quite a bit of the skin can be used as a sacrificial layer.
—Nicolai

Light the fire, let it burn to embers, and place the potatoes directly onto the embers.

Turn the potatoes now and then while they are cooking. Cooking time depends on their size, but give them at least 40 minutes. The potatoes should succumb to pressure and feel quite tender when stuck with a knife.

Remove the potatoes from the embers, divide them into halves, and serve immediately—the burnt outer layer should not be eaten.

PEACHES

SMOKED WITH ROSEMARY

Log cabin, lean-to, or hunter's fire

5–6

Grill rack

SERVES 4

- 1 bunch of rosemary
- 4 peaches
- salt
- olive oil

On the border between Slovenia and Italy, our friends Simona and Alex live on a wine estate, where the noble art of wine making has been passed down for generations. Besides being one of the most beautiful places I know, it is also the place I dream of being reborn. Among grapevines as far as the eye reaches, you will stumble upon an occasional peach tree, and rosemary bushes as tall as houses. They inspired me to cook this dish, which I made for my 40th birthday at Simona and Alex's home. It's a super-simple dish and a great combination of ingredients to enjoy with amazing company.
—Nicolai

Light the fire and let it burn to embers. Meanwhile, immerse the rosemary in water for a minimum of 15 minutes. Position the grill rack about 8 inches (20 cm) above the embers.

Cut the peaches in half and remove the stones. Grill the peaches with the cut side down and place the rosemary sprigs directly in the embers so that they start to smoke. Grill the peaches for about 5 minutes. Season with salt and sprinkle with olive oil.

Serve with sprigs of the still-smoking rosemary. These are not to be eaten but to complement the sensory experience with a beautiful rosemary aroma.

PEAS

WITH AIOLI

Log cabin or lean-to fire

8

SERVES 2–4

- 8 cups (½ kg) fresh peas in the pod
- 1 egg
- 2 cloves of garlic, grated
- juice of ½ lemon
- 1 tsp. salt
- about ¾ cup (200 ml) grapeseed oil
- 2 tbsp. olive oil

Light the fire and let it burn to calm embers.

Place the pea pods in the embers and cook for 5–7 minutes, or until they are just starting to turn black.

Beat the egg and add grated garlic, lemon juice, and salt. Whip everything together, and then add the combined oils in a thin stream while constantly whipping. Continue until the oil is completely emulsified. Add a bit more salt or lemon juice if needed.

Remove the pea pods from the embers and open them halfway. Spoon a dab of aioli into each pod, and serve.

TOMATOES

WITH WOODRUFF

Log cabin, lean-to, teepee, or hunter's fire

5–6

Coarse-mesh sieve, grill rack

SERVES 2–4

- 3 cloves of garlic, finely chopped
- 1–2 sprigs of fresh thyme, finely chopped
- 2 cups (500 ml) olive oil
- 20 cherry tomatoes, multicolored
- 3 beefsteak tomatoes
- 1 tbsp. apple vinegar (see p. 249)
- 1 tbsp. sugar
- salt
- 1 bunch of woodruff

Light the fire and let it burn to embers.

Mix the chopped garlic and thyme with olive oil. Toss with the cherry tomatoes. Place the cherry tomatoes in a sieve.

Put a fresh piece of firewood on the fire so that it starts to smoke. Hold the sieve over the embers and smoke. Shake the sieve gently until the skins of the tomatoes begin to burst. At this point, do not shake the sieve anymore but simply hold it over the smoke and embers until the tomatoes collapse slightly, about 10 minutes. Then put the cherry tomatoes in a bowl and season with salt.

Place a grill rack about 6 inches (15 cm) over the embers.

Cut the beefsteak tomatoes in half and season the cut side with vinegar, sugar, and a bit of salt. Grill them on the grill rack (cut-side down) for 5 minutes, until they have developed quite a bit of color. Place the grilled beefsteak tomatoes on a platter with the cherry tomatoes. Garnish with fresh woodruff, and serve.

BURNT CARROTS

WITH SMOKED HOLLANDAISE & LOVAGE

Log cabin
or lean-to fire

8–9

SERVES 4

- 2 bundles of fresh carrots with tops
- 1 cup (250 g) smoked butter (see p. 257)
- 2 egg yolks
- 2 tbsp. apple vinegar (see p. 249)
- 1 tsp. salt
- 1 bunch of lovage

Light the fire and let it burn to fire strength 8–9. Remove their tops, place the carrots in the embers, and let them cook for about 20 minutes.

Meanwhile, heat the smoked butter in a saucepan and toss the egg yolks into another saucepan. Add apple vinegar and salt to the egg yolks and whisk them over the heat from the fire until the mixture is thick and creamy. Remove the saucepan from the heat and gradually add the melted smoked butter while constantly whipping. When all the butter is absorbed, add salt and vinegar to taste.

Remove the carrots from the embers and rub off their burnt peels. Place them on a platter, top with some smoked hollandaise, and garnish with lovage leaves.

CORN
À LA OAXACA

Log cabin, lean-to, or hunter's fire

7–8

Cord, fire tongs

SERVES 2

- 2 corncobs
- 4 tbsp. crème fraîche, 38% fat
- salt
- 1 ¾ oz. (50 g) Parmesan cheese
- 1 tsp. spicy paprika

This way of cooking corn is my take on a classic of Mexican street food that's traditionally served on a stick with cotija cheese and chili powder.
—Nicolai

Light the fire and let it burn to calm embers.

Meanwhile, tie the corncobs' leaves tightly to them with cord and soak them in water. The cord will prevent them from opening when soaking. Keep them in the water for at least 15 minutes, preferably 1 hour.

When the embers are ready, place the corncobs directly onto them and cook for 10–15 minutes. Turn them occasionally with tongs and let the outer leaves burn. Remove the corncobs from the embers and let them cool slightly. Bend the leaves away from the corn and remove the corn silk.

Spread crème fraîche over each cob, drizzle with salt, finely grate fresh Parmesan over the top, and sprinkle with paprika.

GRILLED ZUCCHINI

WITH RAMSON & FRIED EGG

Log cabin
or lean-to fire

5–6

Grill rack,
flat coarse-mesh sieve

SERVES 4

- 2 zucchinis
- olive oil
- juice of ½ lemon
- salt
- 4 eggs
- 10 ramson leaves and flowers

Light the fire and let it burn to hot embers. Place a grill rack over the embers and let it get very warm.

Cut the zucchini horizontally into 1⁄10 inch (3 mm) slices and grill them on both sides until cooked and well colored, about 5 minutes.

Place the zucchini slices in a bowl and season with olive oil, lemon juice, and salt to taste.

Roll each ramson leaf into a tight roll and cut into fine, long strips that you'll save for later.

Make the fried eggs as follows: Place a grill rack about 8 inches (20 cm) above the embers. Lubricate the flat sieve with a bit of olive oil and place it on the grill rack. Crack the eggs into the sieve, keeping the yolks unbroken. The viscosity of the eggs will prevent them from draining through the holes in the sieve, and at the same time the eggs will absorb heat and smoke, developing a smoky taste and scent. Remove the eggs from the sieve by sliding a spatula underneath. Season with salt.

Place the fried eggs on a plate and arrange the zucchini and finely chopped ramson around them. Decorate with the ramson flowers, and serve.

SMOKED JERUSALEM ARTICHOKE SOUP

Keyhole fire

5–6

Bonfire stand, 6-quart (6-liter) Dutch oven, ember shovel, coarse-mesh sieve, cloth

SERVES 4

- 1 chicken
- 2 yellow onions
- 1 clove of garlic
- 1 carrot
- 1 parsnip
- 2–3 bay leaves
- 1 tbsp. black peppercorns
- 14 oz. (400 g) Jerusalem artichokes
- 1 lemon
- salt

Light the fire and let it burn to embers. Scrape the embers out to one side and feed the fire with more firewood.

Put the chicken directly onto the embers and grill it until it is dark and fried all over, turning frequently. Place the chicken in the Dutch oven and hang the pot on the campfire stand over the embers. Fill it to just below the brim with water.

Wash but do not peel the onions, garlic, carrot, and parsnip and cut into coarse pieces. Add the vegetables to the Dutch oven along with bay leaves and peppercorns. Bring the broth to a boil once, then adjust the embers so that you find a point where the soup can simmer without boiling heavily. It should simmer for a minimum of 3 hours (without a lid), so feed your campfire with more firewood and add new embers under the Dutch oven with your shovel regularly.

Cut the washed Jerusalem artichokes into halves and place them in the sieve. Put a fresh piece of firewood on the embers so that it starts to smoke. Grill/smoke the Jerusalem artichokes until they are golden in color.

When the broth has simmered for 3 hours, strain it and then bring to a boil. Add the Jerusalem artichokes while the broth is boiling. Take the Dutch oven off the heat, put on the lid, and wrap it in a cloth. Let the broth infuse with the Jerusalem artichokes for 2 hours.

Strain the artichokes from the broth and set them aside. Cook the broth until half of the liquid has evaporated. Cut the lemon into halves and grill (cut-side down) on a grill rack. Season with salt and juice from the grilled lemon, add the Jerusalem artichokes to the soup, and serve.

SMASHING PUMPKIN

ASIAN STYLE

Log cabin, lean-to, or hunter's fire

6–8

Rotisserie (or 1 skewer of about 3 feet / 1 m and 2 Y-shaped sticks), mortar

SERVES 4

- 1 Hokkaido pumpkin
- 1 red chili
- 1 tsp. coriander seeds
- 1 small tuber of ginger
- 1 stalk of lemongrass, ripped into pieces
- 2 cloves of garlic
- 1 tbsp. sesame oil
- 1 tsp. brown sugar
- juice of 1 lime
- 1 handful of cilantro
- 1 handful of edible flowers, such as marigold or nasturtium
- salt
- olive oil

Light the fire and let it burn to embers.

Place the pumpkin on a skewer or rotisserie and bake it over the embers until completely tender and almost falling apart, about 1 hour. Be sure to turn it almost constantly so that the outside becomes golden and crisp without burning.

Meanwhile, grind together the chili, coriander seeds, ginger, lemongrass, and garlic in a mortar. Add the sesame oil, brown sugar, and lime juice, and stir until you have a coarse marinade.

Gently split the hot pumpkin and remove the kernels. Break the pumpkin into coarse pieces and pour the marinade over them. Sprinkle with cilantro and edible flowers.

Give the salad a good sprinkle of salt and a small drizzle of olive oil, and serve immediately.

SEAFOOD

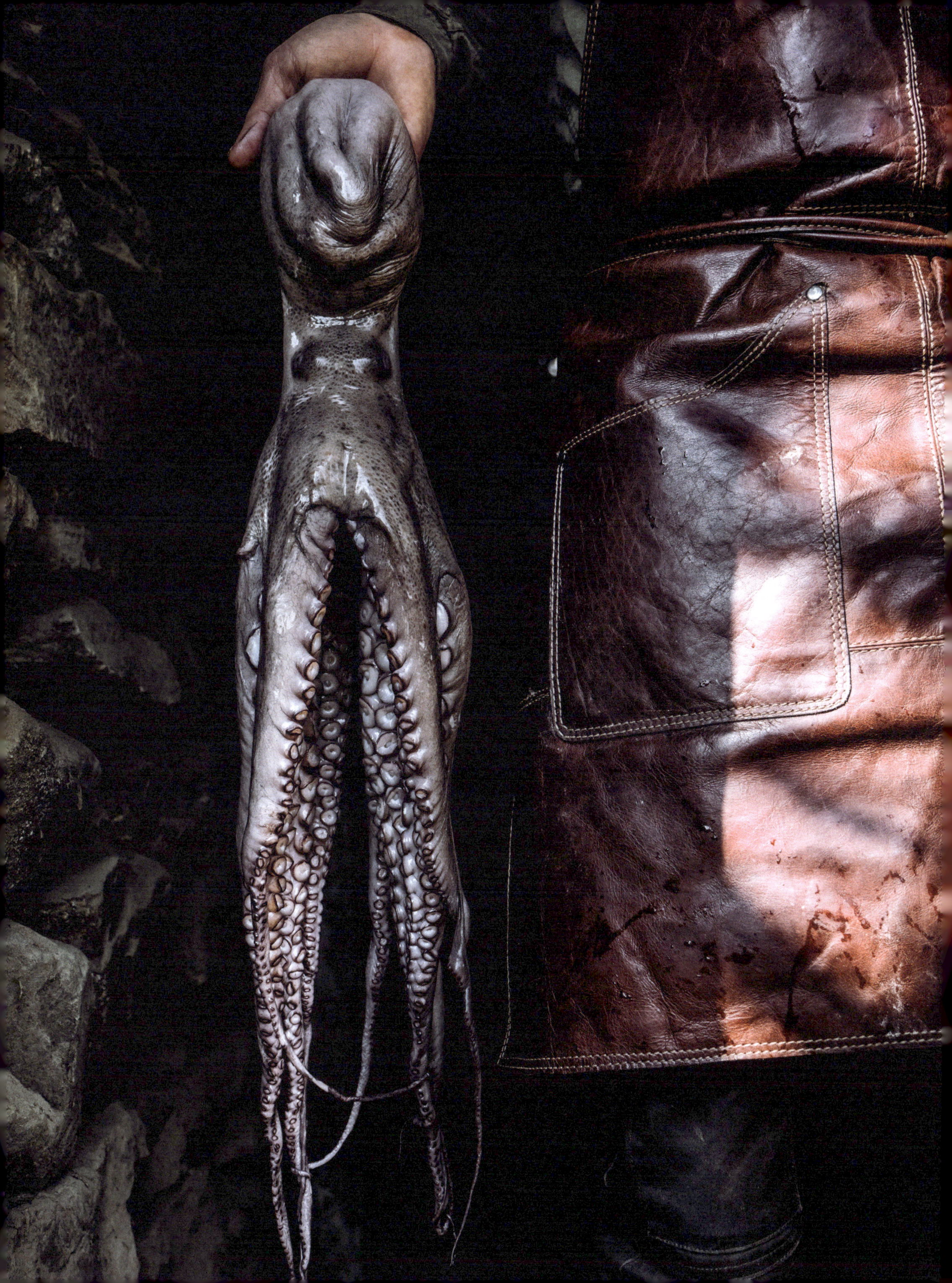

SEA TROUT

"ASADO"

Log cabin, lean-to, or teepee fire

3–4

1 short stick, about ¾ inch (2 cm) in diameter and 8 inches (20 cm) long, 2 long sticks, 2–2 ¾ inches (5–7 cm) in diameter and 3 feet (1 m) long, thin wire, pliers

SERVES 6

- 1 handful of parsley
- 5 cloves of garlic
- 3 fresh bay leaves
- 1 cup (200 ml) olive oil
- 1 cup (200 ml) water
- 2 tbsp. (30 g) salt
- 2 tsp. white pepper
- 2 bundles of fresh herbs, such as bay leaves, rosemary, chives, or parsley
- 1 large sea trout

Light the fire and let it burn to embers. You should keep the fire burning throughout the cooking process, so make sure you have plenty of firewood ready to feed it as needed.

Make the marinade by thoroughly blending together the handful of parsley, garlic, bay leaves, olive oil, water, salt, and white pepper.

Make a brush by firmly attaching the bundles of fresh herbs to your short stick. Make a cut at the end of one of your long sticks and remove the bark. Remove the bark from the other long stick as well and divide it into 5 equally sized pieces. Tie the 5 smaller pieces to the big stick to make a cross with 10 arms.

Clean the trout, remove the guts, and run a sharp knife along the backbone inside the fish. Cut off the small bones so you can open the fish like a butterfly. Place the fish with the scaly side against the cross and tie it to the sticks by inserting a thin wire through the skin. Use the small, hard pieces of cartilage around the fish's head, abdomen, and tail to secure it. Now push the pointed end of the stick into the ground so that the fish is angled over the fire. It must be angled so that you can hold your hand in front of the trout for 15 seconds without it getting too hot. If you can keep it there for longer, you need to move the fish closer. If you can't hold it there for 15 seconds, move the fish a bit further away.

Dip your brush into the marinade and splash plenty of it all over the fish. Repeat this every 5 minutes for the next 30 minutes while the trout is cooking. The cooking time depends on the size of the fish and the temperature of your fire—break a small piece of meat off once the surface has turned nicely light brown and taste, to check if it is to your liking.

GRILLED OCTOPUS

Keyhole fire

5–6

Campfire stand, grill rack, ember shovel, Dutch oven

SERVES 4

- 1 bunch of parsley
- 3 red onions
- 1 head of garlic
- 1 wine cork
- 1 tbsp. black peppercorns
- 1 clove
- 1 octopus
- olive oil
- 2 lemons
- salt

The ingredient list for this dish includes a wine cork, which may seem strange. It's an old wives' tale that the cork makes the octopus more tender. I have never tried to cook octopus without one, so I don't know if it's just a myth or is actually true! But it does no harm, so why not? —Nicolai

Light the fire and put the campfire stand next to it. Once the embers are ready, use the shovel to push them under the campfire stand. Feed your fire with more firewood. Hang the Dutch oven with 5 ¼ quarts (5 liters) of water from the campfire stand above the embers. When the water is boiling, add parsley, halved red onions and garlic, the wine cork, black peppercorns, and the clove.

Cut the head off the octopus right under the eyes. Slide your finger through the hole to pop the beak out of the octopus's mouth. Rinse thoroughly under cold water. Hold the octopus with its arms down, dip it into the water three times, and place it completely under the water on the fourth dip (the dips make the arms curl up nicely). Let the octopus cook for 1–1 ½ hours. Check the tenderness by poking a knife into the arms.

When the octopus is tender, lift it onto a cutting board and divide it into arms. Now you can one of do two things: either scrape off the dark red skin or leave it on. The skin contains a lot of collagen, and some people find it a bit slimy. I think it tastes really good when it's almost burned on the grill. If you keep the skin on, pour some oil over the octopus—otherwise it will stick to whatever it touches.

Remove the campfire stand and place a grill rack over the hot embers, split the lemons and grill them until dark on the cut side.

Lay the octopus arms on the grill until they gain plenty of color. Grill them on both sides and place on a platter. Place the lemons on the side, sprinkle with salt, and serve.

SALMON SKEWERS

Log cabin, lean-to, or hunter's fire

5–6

6 thin spruce branches, free from needles and bark at one end

SERVES 2

- ¼ cup (50 g) rosehip petal vinegar (see p. 251) or apple vinegar (see p. 249)
- 1 cup (200 ml) strong chicken stock
- 1 cup (200 ml) beet juice
- 1 tbsp. black peppercorns
- 1 tbsp. mustard seeds
- 14 oz. (400 g) salmon fillet
- flaky salt

Light the fire and wait for the flames to burn out. You want hot embers without the flames, as they will cover your salmon in soot.

In a saucepan, reduce the vinegar by half. Add chicken stock and beet juice to the reduced vinegar along with peppercorns and mustard seeds. Let the liquid boil for about 15 minutes, then sieve the sauce to remove the peppercorns and mustard seeds. Let the glaze simmer until it has a honey-like consistency. It's important to keep an eye on it, because it can quickly go from perfect to at risk of burning.

Cut the salmon into 6 strips about 1 ½–2 inches (4–5 cm) in length and stick the spruce branches through them. Grill them over the embers until they turn a nice color all over. Brush them all over with the glaze and quickly grill again so that the glaze caramelizes. Finally, sprinkle a little flaky salt on top, and serve.

STUFFED SQUID

WITH BEANS & PIMENT D'ESPELETTE

Log cabin, lean-to, or hunter's fire

5–6

3 toothpicks

SERVES 2

- 1 squid, about 10–11 ¾ inches (25–30 cm) in cape
- 2 slices of white bread
- ⅓ cup (75 ml) whole milk
- olive oil
- 3 cloves of garlic
- 1 banana shallot
- ½ cup (100 g) cooked white beans
- ½ cup (75 ml) Manzanilla sherry
- salt
- juice and zest of 1 lemon
- 1 tsp. piment d'Espelette (or dried chili)
- 1 handful of coarsely cut bronze fennel

Working on this book has given us some fun experiences we wouldn't have had without it, such as the afternoon we spent at our local lake beach grilling squid. Our children were off from school and came along with us. It was November, and I can attest that we were the only ones who'd gotten the idea to go to the beach. But what an afternoon we had. We laughed, ate squid, and one of our boys, of course, came home with a wet sock. I came home with a full heart.
—Eva

Light the fire and let it burn to hot embers.

Meanwhile, prepare the squid. Pull off the arms, pull out the guts, and cut off the head just below the beak. Cut the arms into rough pieces. Rinse the inside of the squid thoroughly and pull out the large, plastic-like bone (the quill).

Break the bread into pieces and leave it to soak in the milk. Set it aside.

Prepare the filling: Roast the roughly cut arms in olive oil until they get a bit of color to them, then add finely sliced garlic and shallot. Roast a bit more, add the beans, and toss well. Add the sherry and bring it to a boil. Turn down the heat and let the pot simmer while stirring every now and then until the sherry has evaporated. Complete the filling by adding the soaked bread, and season with salt, lemon juice and zest, and piment d'Espelette.

Pour the stuffing into a piping or plastic bag and use to fill the squid with stuffing. Close the hole in the squid's cape with the toothpicks. When the embers are ready, place the stuffed squid directly on them and roast for 6–8 minutes, turning frequently.

Take the squid out of the fire and cut into 5–6 large slices. Sprinkle with bronze fennel, salt, a bit of lemon juice, and serve.

SCALLOPS

WITH HAZELNUTS & LEMON THYME

Log cabin, lean-to, or hunter's fire

4–5

Pliers, steel wire, coarse-mesh sieve

SERVES 2–4

- 4 fresh scallops in the shell
- 1 cup (200 g) butter
- 3–4 tbsp. apple vinegar (see p. 249)
- 24 hazelnuts
- salt
- 1 handful of lemon thyme

Light the fire and let it burn to embers.

Meanwhile, prepare the scallops. Force a knife in under the flat shell and let it run along the shell until you hit the scallop. Cut the scallop free from the top of the shell and open the shell. Now cut the scallop free from the bottom of the shell and wash away the roe and intestines under cold water. When the scallops are nice and clean, place them on a plate. Wash the shells with cold water.

Now make your browned butter: Put the butter in a saucepan and place the saucepan in the fire. Let the butter sizzle so the whey starts to fry. When the whey seems dark and the clear part of the butter has changed color from yellow to light brown, remove from the heat and sieve away the whey. Add the apple vinegar to the butter and keep it warm.

Place the hazelnuts in a sieve and roast them over the embers until golden in color.

Now assemble the dish: Place a scallop in each of the curved shell halves, and season with salt. Arrange hazelnuts around each scallop and add 2 spoonfuls of browned-butter vinaigrette and a few sprigs of lemon thyme. Lay the flatter half of shell on top of each scallop and tie the halves together with steel wire. Tighten the steel wire with your pliers so that the edges are completely tight.

Place the scallops in the fire for 5–7 minutes, then take them out and serve immediately. Serve with the pliers on the table and let guests open the scallops themselves and enjoy the delicious aroma when they are freshly opened.

"When I was a child, my parents had a cottage in Blokhus on Denmark's North Sea coast. I can still smell the scent of rosehip blending with the salty breeze from the sea and campfire smoke. I remember the feeling of being scratched by lyme grass on my legs as I walked through the dunes down to the beach to take a swim. How German tourists in motor homes lit campfires, shielded from the North Sea's strong winds behind colored windscreens stretched out between the camper and an aluminum stick knocked into the sand. This dish tastes and smells of rosehip, saltwater, and smoke, and sends me straight back to Blokhus in 1987."

—Nicolai

OYSTERS & PEARLS

Log cabin, lean-to, teepee, or hunter's fire

7–8

SERVES 2

- 1 tbsp. tapioca pearls
- ¾ cup (200 ml) rosehip petal vinegar and some pickled rosehip petals (see p. 251)
- 1 shallot
- 4 oysters

Light the fire and let it burn to embers.

Begin with the tapioca pearls. Boil them in plenty of water until you can just see the little white ball in the middle of the pearls, about 10–12 minutes. Sift off the water with a sieve. Spoon the pearls into half of the rosehip petal vinegar and leave them for at least 1 hour, preferably overnight.

Peel and dice the shallot as finely as possible. Toss the diced shallot into another bowl, with the remaining rosehip petal vinegar.

When the embers are ready, place the oysters directly onto them, and leave them until they open. Sometimes this happens fast and at other times takes a while, but don't stress over them; they will open eventually. As soon as they open, lift them out, and cut them free from the two muscles, in the top and bottom shells, respectively. Turn each oyster upside down and smell to check if it's fresh, discarding any that isn't. Remove any shell fragments and impurities with a knife.

Place some pearls and diced shallot on each oyster. Finally, top each with a rosehip petal, and serve.

HANGED MACKERELS

Log cabin, lean-to, or teepee fire

2 sticks, about 1 ½ feet (50 cm) long and as thick as a thumb

3 – 4

MAKES 2 PIECES

- 2 tbsp. (30 g) salt
- 2 tbsp. (30 g) sugar
- 2 dressed mackerels

Light the fire and feed it continuously with firewood to keep it always at fire strength 3 – 4.

Mix together the salt and sugar and sprinkle all over the mackerels—inside and out. Leave them to absorb the salt and sugar for about 30 minutes.

Hammer the sticks into the ground so that they are positioned at about a 70-degree angle, which will allow the mackerels to hang from their "chins" in front of the flames. You should be able to hold your hand directly in front of them for 15 seconds without getting burned. Be sure to keep the fire smoking by adding fresh firewood or leaves at regular intervals. Depending on their size, the mackerels should hang for about 30 – 45 minutes. You can check one for doneness by opening the belly a little. If it feels warm, they are ready.

CRAB CLAWS

WITH PICKLED CICELY

Log cabin or lean-to fire

5–6

Grill rack

SERVES 2

- 1 tbsp. cicely seeds (or fennel seeds)
- ½ cup (100 ml) apple vinegar (see p. 249)
- 8 crab claws
- 1 handful of chopped licorice-flavored herbs, such as cicely, bronze fennel, or Spanish chervil

The pickled cicely seeds should be prepared at least a couple of weeks in advance, but once done they will last for years. Just take a handful of cicely capsules, put them in a small jar, pour the vinegar over them, and leave them in the refrigerator until you are ready to use them.

Light your fire and let it burn to embers. Put a grill rack over embers and let it heat well.

Hit the top of each claw with the back of a spoon so the shell breaks slightly. Grill the claws for 15 minutes and place them in a dish.

Arrange with the pickled cicely capsules and fresh herbs.

COD
EN PAPILLOTE

Log cabin or lean-to fire | 8–9 | Stone, baking paper

SERVES 2

- 2 egg whites
- 2 cod fillets, about 3 ½ oz. (100 g) each
- 1 tbsp. butter
- 1 lemon
- 8 small carrots
- 6 fresh pea pods
- 10 small new potatoes
- 1 bunch of chervil
- salt

Light the fire and find a large, dry stone to put into it. The stone must be dry, because a wet stone can burst when water that has found its way inside the stone evaporates when exposed to high temperature.

Place a piece of baking paper on the table and brush all over with the egg whites. Top with a new piece of baking paper and let the egg whites stick the sheets together.

At the center of the top sheet and slightly to one side, place one cod fillet to start creating a small packet. Dollop a bit of butter onto the fillet, sprinkle with salt, and top with a slice of lemon. Place 4 carrots on top of the cod. Remove the peas from three of the pods and sprinkle them into the packet. Depending on their size, cut the potatoes into halves or quarters, to about the size of half an olive. Finally, add a few sprigs of chervil.

Brush the edges of the baking paper with more egg white and fold each of the long sides over the fish until the edges meet in the center of the packet. Fold the edges inward, as you would for a calzone. Brush the seam with egg whites to prevent the packet from opening. Repeat with the second cod fillet.

Place the packets on the hot stone in the embers and let them puff up. Then turn the packets over and let them cook about 4–5 minutes. Let your guest open the package themselves, with a sharp knife or scissors, to enjoy the wonderful aroma as it's released.

LOBSTER

WITH HIBISCUS

Log cabin, lean-to, or hunter's fire

5–6

SERVES 1–2

- 2 tbsp. dried hibiscus flowers
- ½ cup (100 ml) apple vinegar (see p. 249)
- 1 egg
- 1 tsp. salt
- ¾ cup (200 ml) grapeseed oil
- 2 tbsp. olive oil
- 1 black lobster
- 1 large handful of wood sorrel (or another citrusy herb)

Light the fire and let it burn to hot embers.

Meanwhile, make a hibiscus mayonnaise: Place the dried hibiscus leaves in the vinegar until soft, about 10 minutes. Finely chop the hibiscus flowers and place in a bowl with a tablespoon of the vinegar. Add the egg and salt and whisk the mixture together. Add the oil a little at a time while constantly whisking until the oil is completely absorbed. Add more salt and vinegar to taste.

Kill the lobster by cutting through the head. Place it directly into the embers for 7 minutes: 3 minutes on the stomach and 4 minutes on the back. Remove the lobster from the embers and let it cool down slightly. Break off the tail and claws, and split the head with your knife. Clean the content from each half of the head and replace with a large spoonful of hibiscus mayonnaise. Top with wood sorrel. Split the tail, remove the intestines, and bash the claws with your knife so that the shell is slightly crushed and can be torn apart easily when serving.

BLUE MUSSELS

"ÉCLADE DE MOULES"

SERVES 2–4

- 2 ¼ lbs. (1 kg) blue mussels
- 1 armful of dry hay

This recipe originates from La Rochelle in southwestern France and is traditionally made on the beach. A large number of mussels is covered with hay and pine needles, which is then ignited. The heat steams the mussels while the smoke gives them a hearty aroma. In other words, you do not need a campfire for this recipe.

Wash the mussels under running water. Any beards should be pulled off. Broken and open mussels should be discarded.

Place a large mussel in the middle of a heat-proof dish. Lean the mussels against each other so that all of the mussels eventually stand upright in a spiral and support each other.

Cover the mussels with a pile of hay. Make sure the hay is not packed too tightly; it should be possible for oxygen to get in. Ignite the hay and let it burn out. When the mussels start to make small puffing sounds, that is your sign that they are being cooked.

Blow off the burnt hay and eat the mussels directly from the shells.

SALMON

"LOIMULOHI"

Teepee, log cabin, or lean-to fire

3–4

1 plank, 2 feet × 12 inches (25 × 60 cm), preferably pine (other wood types can be used), 1 fresh stick (thick as a finger), 1 drill and a drill bit slightly thinner than the stick, camping knife

SERVES 4

- 1 side of salmon, skin on
- ½ cup (100 ml) brandy
- 2 tbsp. sugar
- 2 tbsp. salt

Loimulohi *is Finnish for "blazed," and this is how the Finns traditionally cook salmon.*

Start by making the *loimulohi* plank: Place the salmon on the board with the skin side down, take note of its size (or trace around it with a pencil), and pick it up again. Now drill 5–6 holes into the board and place the salmon back on the board (with the skin side down again). Cut the stick into 6 "nails" of 2 ¼ – 2 ¾ inch (6–7 cm) in length and pare them with your knife to make slightly pointed ends. Punch the nails straight through the salmon so that the skin is perforated and the salmon is fastened in place.

Light the fire and let it burn up into flames. Feed it regularly to maintain this fire strength.

Place the plank with the salmon in front of the fire at such a distance that you can hold one hand in front of it for about 15 seconds without getting burned.

Stir the brandy, sugar, and salt together and pour a few spoonfuls over the salmon every now and then. After about 15 minutes turn the board 180 degrees, to ensure that the salmon is evenly cooked. It should cook for 30–40 minutes, depending on the size.

HALIBUT

"FLAMBADOU"

Log cabin, lean-to, teepee, or hunter's fire

5–6

Flambadou

SERVES 2

- 3 ½ oz. (100 g) halibut fillet
- 1 green apple
- olive oil
- salt
- 1 small bunch of chives
- 2 ½ tbsp. (30 g) lard
- edible flowers

Flambadou is a method of cooking that dates back to the Middle Ages and looks pretty cool. You take a wrought-iron cone with a hole in the bottom, which is placed in the fire until it is red hot, after which lard or butter is added and ignited. The fat burns and drips slowly from the hole, ensuring that the meat below is cooked only on the outside, with a nice, grilled taste, while the inside remains juicy.

Light the fire and let it burn to hot embers. Place the flambadou in the embers and let it turn red-hot.

Cut the halibut fillet into thin slices and spread them out on a dish. Cut the apple into cubes, place the cubes in a bowl, and toss with 1 tbsp. olive oil and season with salt. Cut the chives into fine rings. Distribute apple cubes and chives on top of the cod.

Take the flambadou out of the embers and add in the lard. Now place the flambadou over the embers and ignite the lard immediately. Remove the flambadou and hold it above the fish to let the burning fat drizzle over the fish so that it is quickly fried on the top, leaving a thin layer of golden fat. Arrange with edible flowers (I used apple flowers). I recommend eating this dish with your hands.

LANGOUSTINES

WITH CITRUS HERBS

Log cabin, lean-to, or hunter's fire

5

Grill rack, grill brush

SERVES 2

- 1 lemon and its zest
- 4 langoustines
- olive oil
- salt
- 1 small bunch of lemon balm
- 1 small bunch of lemon verbena
- 1 small bunch of lemon thyme

Light the fire and let it burn to warm embers. Place a grill rack so that it is 2 inches (5 cm) above the embers. Let the grill rack heat up for 5 minutes. Brush thoroughly with the grill brush to ensure that it is completely clean. Split the lemon and rub the cut side against the grill rack to remove all impurities.

Place one langoustine on its back on a cutting board and use a bread knife to split it from head to tail, but do not cut through the shell on the back. Crack the shell on the langoustine's front with your hands so that it opens and exposes the meat, but do not pull the back apart. Take out the black intestine and discard. Repeat with all the langoustines.

Place the langoustines on the grill rack with the meat side toward the embers and grill for 1–2 minutes, depending on their size. Remove from the grill and place them on their backs. Drizzle with olive oil and sprinkle with salt.

Wash the herbs and make small bouquets of them. Toss them in a bit of olive oil, salt, and lemon zest, and arrange a small bouquet of lemon herbs on each langoustine.

Serve the dish without cutlery, as it is best eaten with the hands.

GRILLED PLAICE

WITH LEMON & ROSEMARY

Log cabin, lean-to, teepee, or hunter's fire

5–6

2 grill nets

SERVES 2

- 2 plaice
- 1 lemon
- 4–6 sprigs of rosemary
- salt
- olive oil

Light the fire and let it burn to hot embers.

Cut the head off the plaice and cut the fins off with scissors. Peel off the dark skin by loosening some of it at the head and holding onto it with a towel. Pull the skin toward the tail and all the way off. Remove any blood from the abdomen and rinse thoroughly.

Cut the lemon into 6–8 slices. Place each fish on a grill net with a few lemon slices and rosemary sprigs. Close the net and squeeze it to keep everything together. Sprinkle the plaice with salt, drizzle with olive oil, and grill directly in the embers for 3 minutes on each side.

MEAT

GRILLED ENTRECÔTE

WITH GARLIC & THYME

Log cabin, lean-to, or hunter's fire

5

Grill rack, Dutch oven

SERVES 4

- 5 cloves of garlic
- 1 bunch of thyme
- 1 quart (1 l) olive oil
- 1 entrecôte, 18 oz. (500 g) in weight
- salt and pepper

Start 3 days in advance. Make the marinade, first crushing all the garlic cloves with the back of your hand; put them in a bowl. Rinse the thyme thoroughly and place it in the bowl with the garlic. Pour the oil over them, and spread the thyme and garlic out in the oil with a spoon. Place the meat in a container or dish, and pour the marinade over it. Allow the meat to marinate for 3 days in the refrigerator.

Light the fire and let it burn to fire strength 5. Place a grill rack about 4 inches (10 cm) above the embers.

Remove the meat from the marinade and dry it, ensuring that it's free of any lingering oil. Place it on the grill rack and season with salt and pepper immediately. Let the meat grill for 1–1½ minutes, turn 45 degrees, and continue to grill. Continue turning the steak every 1–2 minutes, until it is darkly caramelized all over. Turn the steak over and repeat on the other side. Remember to season with salt and pepper on this side as well. Place the steak in the Dutch oven and cover with the lid. Let it stand for 5 minutes.

Take out the meat and place it on a cutting board. Cut it into slices ¼-inch (½-cm) thick. Serve immediately with the pan gravy on the side.

STICKY RIBS

Log cabin, lean-to, or hunter's fire

6–7

Grill rack, campfire stand, Dutch oven, brush

SERVES 4

- 2 racks of pork spareribs
- 1 onion, split
- 1 clove of garlic
- 1 handful of black peppercorns
- 3 bay leaves
- 2 star anise
- 2 tbsp. flower honey
- ½ cup (100 ml) mirin (sweet rice wine)
- 1 cup (200 ml) soy sauce
- 3 tsp. red curry paste

Light the fire and let it burn to embers.

Put the spareribs in the Dutch oven and cover them with water. Add the split onion and garlic (keep the peel on). Add peppercorns, bay leaves, and star anise and hang the pot on your campfire stand over the embers. Bring the pot to a boil, and adjust your embers so the ribs can simmer for a couple of hours.

Prepare your glaze by boiling honey, mirin, soy sauce, and curry paste until it is almost burning. The longer you dare to cook it, the better it will be.

When the spareribs have cooked for a couple of hours, remove the pot from the heat. Add some more firewood to the fire and let it burn to fire strength 6.

Put a grill rack over the embers and take the ribs out of the pot, but be careful, as they are very tender and fall apart easily. Grill the ribs until they are well colored, then brush them on both sides with the glaze a few times. Let them grill a bit more, but be cautious, because at this stage they burn easily. They should be grilled only until just caramelized.

PORK SHANK

IN SALT DOUGH

Keyhole or log cabin fire

5–9

Gloves, ember shovel, pitchfork

SERVES 4

- 8 cups (1 kg) wheat flour
- 3 ½ cups (1 kg) fine salt
- 7 ¾ oz. (220 g) egg whites
- 1 ¼ – 1 ⅔ cups (300 – 400 ml) water
- 1 pork shank
- 4 tbsp. coarse mustard
- 1 bunch of tarragon

Wrapping meat in a salt dough is a method of preparation that can be used for many different types of meat that need to cook for a long time—and large vegetables for that matter. Try it out for yourself and find your favorites.

Light the fire and let it burn to embers. You will need lots of embers, so be generous with the firewood—for this recipe I made a log cabin fire with 14 pieces of firewood.

Make the salt dough by mixing flour and salt with the egg whites. Knead the water into the mixture and continue to knead until the dough has the consistency of wax. Let the dough rest for 1 hour.

Smear the pork shank all over with the mustard. Wash and pick the leaves off the tarragon and "stick" them to the shank.

Divide the dough into 2 halves and sprinkle flour on the table. Roll out one of the halves to ¾ inch (1 ½ cm) in thickness and place the pork shank on top of it. Roll out the other dough half to the same thickness and place it over the shank. Massage the dough to get rid of any air bubbles and squeeze it tightly around the shank. Watch out for small holes and take some dough from other, thicker places to close the holes. Wet your hands and even out the dough.

Put the pork shank—now well wrapped in salt dough—directly onto the embers. Put on gloves and cover the dough with the embers using your shovel. Set your alarm clock to 3 hours, cross your fingers, and hope for the best.

There is nothing more you can do now. The dough turns black as coal and you will be thinking "this is no good," but the pork shank is just fine. The salt dough acts as a cross between a frying pan and a pressure cooker—and when, after 3 hours, you put the shank on the table and punch a hole in the dough, a scent that will entice even the most committed vegetarian will sweep around the table.

MINCEMEAT PATTIES

Log cabin, lean-to, or hunter's fire

6

Grill rack, grill brush

MAKES 2 PIECES

- 14 oz. (400 g) ox chuck
- 1 tsp. ground cumin
- 1 tsp. smoked paprika
- salt and pepper

Light the fire and let the flames burn out so only the hot embers are left.

With a knife, first cut the ox chuck into slices, then into strips and finally into fine cubes—the smaller the better. Spread the meat out on the cutting board and sprinkle with cumin, smoked paprika, salt, and pepper. Gather the mincemeat and press it together so that the small cubes mold together. Divide the mincemeat into 2 balls and form round patties with a thickness of about ¾ inch (2 cm).

Place the grill rack about 8 inches (20 cm) above the embers. Let it heat well for 5 minutes. Then brush it with your grill brush to make sure it is completely clean. If you prefer a smoky flavor, then now add a piece of fresh firewood on one side of the embers, which will immediately produce a lot of smoke and give rise to a nice, smoky taste.

Place the mincemeat patties on the grill and grill them for 2–3 minutes until they have obtained quite a bit of color. Careful: do not turn or move the steak. Resist the temptation to nudge a spatula in under it. At this point, the Maillard reaction has not yet formed the crust on the patty and you'll risk it falling apart.

When the patties are dark and fried on one side, turn them over with a spatula and grill the other side. The same rule applies here: do not touch them until they are done.

When the patties are done on both sides, serve immediately—if desired, as a burger (see p. 198).

CHILI CON CARNE

Log cabin, lean-to, or hunter's fire

5–8

Grill rack, tweezers, Dutch oven, campfire stand

SERVES 6–8

- 2 ¼ lbs. (1 kg) entrecôte
- 1 tbsp. smoked paprika
- 1 tbsp. ground cumin
- 3 red onions
- 3 shallots
- 2 red peppers
- 5 carli peppers
- 4 carrots
- ¼ celeriac
- olive oil
- 4 ¼ oz. (120 g) chorizo sausage
- 5 cloves of garlic
- ¾ cup (150 g) mixed soaked beans
- 1 ¼ cup (300 ml) chicken stock
- ½ cup (100 ml) strong coffee
- 2 tbsp. concentrated tomato puree
- 1 ¾ oz. (50 g) dark chocolate, minimum 60% cocoa
- salt and pepper
- 2–3 different kinds of chili (e.g., piri-piri, habanero, or chipotle)
- 2 cans (14 ½ oz./400 g each) of peeled chopped tomatoes

Light the fire and get it burning nicely. This fire should burn for 4 hours, so you might as well make a big fire right from the start. When the flames start to settle, put the grill rack on.

The following must take place in one long motion: Divide the entrecôte in half and sprinkle it with smoked paprika and cumin, grill it until it has plenty of color, and place it on a cutting board. Cut it into coarse pieces.

Put the onions and shallots onto the embers and let them bake until they appear tender when pressed lightly. Cut the bottom off each and slip the inside out as if you were removing the skin from an almond.

Put the red peppers on the grill rack and burn them completely, then remove them from the fire and peel off the burnt skin with a pair of tweezers. Cut the peppers into rough pieces.

Grill the carli peppers until dark and collapsed. Cut each pepper into 3 pieces across.

Cut the tops off the carrots and split them lengthwise. Grill them cut-side down until they are well colored. Then split them twice more lengthwise. Cut the celeriac into wedges. Grill each wedge on both sides, then cut them into slightly smaller pieces.

Hang the Dutch oven on the campfire stand over the embers and feed the fire with a bit of extra firewood. Add a dash of olive oil to the pot when warm. Add all the grilled ingredients.

Cut the chorizo into ¾-inch (2-cm) thick slices and toss them into the pot. Peel 5 cloves of garlic, crush them with the back of your hand, and toss into the pot. Pour the beans in and add the chicken stock, coffee, tomato puree, and chocolate. Season well with salt and pepper and add the chilies to the pot. Now you must decide how daring you want to be. If you want a grandma-friendly version, you can chop up the chilies and serve them on the side. Add the canned tomatoes and add water until all the ingredients are just covered.

Now let the pot rock over the embers for a minimum of 3 hours, preferably 8, if you can wait that long.

LEG OF LAMB

"CURANTO"

Log cabin, lean-to, or hunter's fire

7

SERVES 4

- 1 leg of lamb with the bone removed, salted overnight
- 5 carrots
- 5 onions
- ½ celeriac
- 1 head of garlic
- salt and pepper
- juice of 1 lemon
- olive oil

Well, I won't lie to you. This recipe is challenging and cumbersome, and it took me quite a few tries to get it right. You have to do curanto *for the fun of it, and you have to be willing to set aside the time that is required. You can use any vegetables and cuts of meat, but the curanto is obviously best suited for things that take time—see below for what I used.*
—Nicolai

Build your *curanto* ("stony ground"): Dig a squarish hole 4 ½ feet (1 ½ m) deep, with sides about 1 ½ feet × 3 feet (½ × 1 m). Fill the bottom of the hole with large stones. Save the soil and collect 10 large stones for later use. In the woods fill a wheelbarrow with fresh branches with needles or leaves. Pull an old sheet out of the closet that you no longer need. Light a huge bonfire at the bottom of the hole. When the fire has burned to embers, throw the stones you have saved onto the embers and let them heat up.

The following should be done in one long motion, the faster the better: Put half of the branches on top of the hot stones. Place the meat, vegetables, and garlic on top of the branches, cover the produce with the rest of the branches, and place the sheet on top. Stretch the sheet out and place stones on the sides so that it does not slip. Pour soil on top—a good, thick layer. Wish yourself luck and do something else for the next 8–10 hours!

Carefully remove the soil until you can see the corners of the sheet. Lift up all corners at the same time so that you catch all the soil. Open the "oven" and enjoy the scent.

Take out the ingredients. Season everything with salt, pepper, olive oil, and lemon juice. Serve the lamb and vegetables as they are, with a sharp knife and a serving spoon.

PORK BREAST

"ASADO"

Log cabin, teepee, or lean-to fire

3–4

Wire, pliers, 2 long sticks, about 3 feet (1 m) in length and 2–2 ¾ inches (5–7 cm) in diameter, 2 Y-shaped sticks

SERVES 8

- 1 pork breast, 6–6 ¾ lbs. (3–4 kg) in weight
- 3 handfuls of salt
- 1 small bunch of parsley
- 5 fresh bay leaves
- 2 tsp. black pepper
- 5 cloves of garlic
- 1 ¼ cups (300 ml) olive oil
- 2 tbsp. (30 g) salt
- 2 cups (500 ml) water
- 1 large bundle of mint

Start a day in advance; it will make a huge difference. Cut the rind of the pork breast into panes. Make sure that you cut all the way through the rind without actually cutting into the meat. Rub the rind with lots of salt. Place the breast with the rind down on a grate so that the salt can pull the water out of the skin (it is the water that prevents the rind from becoming crunchy). Place the grate with the pork breast in the refrigerator overnight.

Light the fire. You will need a nice large campfire, which you'll regularly be adding firewood to. Let the fire burn to strength 3, and prepare the pork breast for cooking in the meantime.

Make an asado cross by removing the bark from one of your long sticks and cutting it so that it's pointy at one end. Remove the bark from the second stick and divide it into 4 pieces of equal length. Fasten the 4 shorter pieces to the long stick to make an asado cross with 8 arms. Tie the pork breast to the cross with the rind side facing out. Be thorough when doing this. You want to have a sense of control when you turn the meat over the campfire—you don't want to worry about whether it will fall off.

Blend the herbs and bay leaves in a blender with pepper, garlic, olive oil, salt, and water—set aside a large bunch of mint, which you will use for making a brush. Find a stick and tie the mint bunch to it so that it looks like a dusting brush.

Sharpen the 2 Y-shaped sticks. Now you are ready to cook. Hammer the pointed end of the asado cross into the ground and tilt so that it is at a 60–70-degree angle from the fire. It should be positioned so that you can hold your hand between the radiant heat from the fire and the meat for about 15 seconds. →

It may be necessary to shorten the pointed stick if the pork breast is too high above the fire. Let the 2 Y-shaped sticks support the cross so that it is stable.

Dip the brush in your marinade and give the pork a few generous lashes. Repeat this process every 30 minutes, turning the pork breast around and letting it cook on the other side. Okay, now you're on your own ... Let me put it this way—your roast should cook for no fewer than 3 hours, but that's all the help I can give you. You have to keep an eye on it and judge for yourself—turn, feel, sense, observe, and swing the brush. How long it needs to cook will depend on the size of your roast, your campfire, the outside temperature, the wind, and how sober you are. But I can guarantee that the result will be outstanding no matter what.

One final trick, however: Just before you serve the meat, lift the cross off the ground and hold the rind straight over the embers, horizontally. It will then start to sizzle and pop. This will give you the best pork crackling you have ever had.

RABBIT

"BLACKENED ASADO"

Log cabin, lean-to, or hunter's fire

5–6

2 sticks about 2–2 ¾ inches (5–7 cm) in diameter and 3 feet (1 m) in length, 1 Y-shaped stick, wire, pliers

SERVES 4

- 1 rabbit
- 2 tbsp. smoked paprika
- 1 handful of thyme
- 10 peppercorns
- 1 tbsp. garlic powder
- 2 tsp. salt
- ½ cup (100 g) butter

The Creole kitchen uses a technique called blackening. It is normally used for fish and was made popular by the Cajun/Creole chef Paul Prudhomme. This recipe combines the Creole approach with the Argentinian cooking technique asado, bringing together the two worlds in a truly delicious way.

Light the fire and let it burn to embers.

Cut one of your sticks to form a point at one end and remove the bark. Remove the bark from the other stick and divide it into 2–3 pieces of equal size. Fasten the 2–3 small pieces to the long stick, using the pliers and wire to create a cross with 4–6 arms.

Tie the rabbit to the cross with wire so that the hind- and forelegs are stretched out.

Grind together the herbs, spices, and salt in a mortar, and melt the butter. Brush the rabbit all over with the melted butter and sprinkle it with the ingredients from the mortar until it is completely red.

Hammer the Y-shaped stick into the ground and lean the stick with the rabbit on it so that it hovers over the embers. Feed the fire with a piece of fresh firewood to create smoke—but make sure that the firewood does not ignite, because then it will cover the rabbit in soot. If the wood is ignited, just move it to the side and let it burn out. Turn the rabbit constantly. It's okay if it gets a few black spots here and there (hence the name), but it should not be burnt. It should cook for 30–40 minutes, but it's better to slightly undercook it rather than overcook it—dry rabbit meat is not very appetizing.

TOMAHAWK

À LA WIENER SCHNITZEL

Log cabin
or lean-to fire

5–6

SERVES 6

- 1 cup (200 g) butter
- 6–7 anchovies
- 1 horseradish
- 1 lemon
- 2 tbsp. capers
- 1 tomahawk steak
- salt and pepper
- a few sprigs of sage

Tomahawk steak, or rib eye on the bone, is a huge steak with a long bone that gives the meat its potency and flavor and makes you think of The Flintstones. *It is protein porn at its finest and will usually make at least one of your guests go, "Wow!"*

Light the fire and let it burn to embers.

Put the butter in a saucepan and the pan on the embers. Let the butter sizzle until the whey starts to fry. When you can see that the whey has turned dark and the clear part of the butter has gone from yellow to light brown in color, remove it from the heat and strain off the whey.

Finely chop the anchovies. Peel the horseradish and scrape it from top to root with a sharp knife. Cut the lemon into slices. Add the lemon and capers to the browned butter. Season the steak generously with salt and pepper and place it directly in the hot embers. Cook for 12–15 minutes in total, flipping it every minute along the way.

Place the steak on a cutting board and let it rest for 5 minutes. Then cover it with the browned-butter mix, add some fresh sage leaves, and serve.

CHICKEN

"FRANGO NO CHURRASCO"

Log cabin, lean-to, or hunter's fire

5–6

Grill rack, grill net

SERVES 4

- 1 chicken
- salt and pepper
- 3 cloves of garlic
- 1 handful of lemon thyme
- juice of 1 lemon
- olive oil
- 1 bunch of tarragon
- 1 handful of pansies (or other edible flowers)

This recipe is inspired by the Portuguese frango no churrasco *recipe, in which you debone the chicken and grill it whole. In other words, you cut the chicken meat from the chicken via the back and therefore end up with a whole chicken hull with no bones. It may seem a bit complicated, but once you get the hang of it, it's really not that difficult. The chicken must be grilled in what the Portuguese call* a grelha*—a grill net in English—which both keeps the chicken in its original shape and makes it easy to cook on both sides.*

Light the fire and let it burn to fire strength 5. Then feed it with 1 or 2 pieces of fresh firewood to create as much smoke as possible.

Meanwhile, place the chicken with the breast down on a cutting board. Make a cut along the backbone from the neck of the chicken down to the rump. Then follow the hull all the way around without cutting through the skin at any point. Make sure to keep your knife close to the hull at all times so that you cut off as little of the meat as possible. At the thighs and wings, make sure to insert the knife into the ball joint and continue cutting. When the chicken meat is freed from the hull, make a cut on the inside of the thigh. Follow the femur with the knife and release the bone from the meat so that the only bone remaining in the chicken is in the lower part of the thigh.

Fold the chicken out so that all the meat is exposed. Season the inside with salt and pepper. You can also add herbs to your taste, garlic, or your favorite marinade at this point. Fold the back again so you get a flat chicken with skin all around. Place the chicken in a grill net and season the skin side with salt and pepper. →

Put a grill rack about 6 inches (15 cm) over the embers and smoking firewood. Place the grill net with the chicken on the grill rack and cook it while turning it around every 3–4 minutes. The chicken should cook like this for about 35–40 minutes, depending on the size.

Finely grate or chop the garlic. Wash, pick, and chop the thyme finely and mix with lemon juice and 3–4 tbsp. olive oil.

Remove the chicken from the fire and drizzle it with the marinade on both sides. Put it back over the embers and allow the marinade to caramelize for a few minutes on each side. Then take the chicken out of the net and let it rest for 5 minutes.

In the meantime, wash the tarragon and scatter it roughly over the chicken. If you're lucky enough to have pansies within reach—or other edible flowers—pick a handful and place them over the chicken. This is mostly just for show, but who doesn't love a meal that looks as good as it tastes?

CHICKEN

"FLAMBADOU"

Log cabin
or lean-to fire

7–8

Cord, 2 Y-shaped sticks about 1 foot (30 cm) long each, 1 rotisserie skewer or a stick as thick as a finger and about 3 ¼ feet (1 m) long, flambadou

SERVES 6–8

- 2 chickens, about 2 ½ lbs. (1,200 g) each
- salt and pepper
- 3 ½ oz. (100 g) lard

Light the fire and let it burn to calm embers.

Meanwhile, prepare the chickens. Loosen the breast skin on each chicken by inserting a finger under the skin. Season with salt and pepper under the skin and also on the outside. Lay each chicken on its stomach and twist the wings toward the back as if you were about to arrest it. Now lay it on its back so the wings are fixed there. Cut about 3 ½ feet (1 m) of cord and hold one end in each hand. Place the cord under the bump of the wings and cross it. Tie a knot so that the bump acts as a fixing point. Pull both ends of the cord up to the breast of the chicken, cross them, and let them pass behind the back and cross again. Finally, pull the cord over the thigh and tie a knot at the fixing point (or wherever feels natural to you—the most important thing is that it's tightened so that it does not hang and flutter when you put it on the skewer). Repeat on the other chicken.

Put the chickens on the skewer and fix them, using the rotisserie clamps or by tying them to the stick with a cord. Hammer the Y-sticks into the ground, one on each side of the campfire. Place the skewer on the Y-sticks and over the embers and add 1 or 2 pieces of firewood so the embers start to smoke. Turn the skewer every 5–10 minutes so that the chickens are cooked evenly all over. They should cook about 1 ½ hours in total.

While they cook, place the flambadou in the embers until it is red-hot. Place a piece of lard in the cone and return the cone to the embers. The lard will ignite. Lift the cone to drip the hot fat from the hole in the bottom over the chickens—pay attention to areas of skin that have not taken color yet. The hot fat from the flambadou will make them turn dark and crispy. Repeat the process several times along the way.

When the chickens are done, remove from the skewer and let them rest for 10 minutes before serving.

GRILLED RACK OF LAMB

WITH ROSEMARY & GARLIC

Log cabin, lean-to, or hunter's fire

5–6

Grill net

SERVES 4

- 2 racks of lamb, about 10 ½ oz. (300 g) each
- 1 bunch of rosemary
- 1 head of garlic
- 2 cups (500 ml) olive oil
- salt and pepper

Start by marinating the meat for as long as possible, preferably for 2 days. Pick the rosemary and crush the garlic with the palm of your hand so that each clove is crushed and exposed. You do not need to remove the peel. Spread the rosemary and garlic around the lamb and cover it completely with olive oil (yes, it is a lot, but the marinade can be reused and kept in the freezer). Allow the lamb to marinate.

Light the fire and let it burn to large embers. Put the lamb in the grill net and season with plenty of salt and pepper. Now hold the lamb as close to the embers as you can without touching them (the oil from the marinade would cause the meat to turn black). As soon as you hear the lamb start to sizzle, turn it over and cook on the other side. Turn the lamb several times. This way you'll get a thick, tasty Maillard reaction on the outside while the lamb remains pink on the inside.

Take the lamb out of the grill net and let it rest for 5 minutes. Cut it into chops with a sharp knife by following the bones.

GRILLED PORK BELLY

WITH HONEY & SOY SAUCE

Log cabin, lean-to, or hunter's fire

5–7

Grill rack

SERVES 2–3

- 1 ¼ cups (300 ml) soy sauce
- ½ cup (100 ml) solid flower honey
- 20 slices of pork belly

Light the fire and let it burn to embers. Position the grill rack about 4 inches (10 cm) above the hot embers and place a saucepan on top. Pour soy sauce and honey into the saucepan, bring to a boil, and let it simmer to reduce some of the liquid.

Meanwhile, grill the pork. The following should be done in one fluid movement: While the marinade is simmering, dip the slices of pork belly in the pan, then put them back on the grill. Grill on both sides, allowing the sugar to caramelize. Repeat, dip and grill. The more you repeat this process, the more flavorful your meat will be. The closer you get to the point where the meat is burnt, the better—it is a very delicate line, and if you cross it, the meat will be ruined. But if you reach this point, the preparation is perfect. Good luck!

BURGERS

WITH COLESLAW & CHIPOTLE BARBECUE SAUCE

Log cabin, lean-to, or hunter's fire

5–8

Coarse-mesh sieve

SERVES 2

- 2 mincemeat patties (see p. 165)
- 2 burger buns (see p. 234)

Coleslaw
- 3 ½ oz. (100 g) white cabbage
- 2 carrots
- 2 egg yolks
- salt
- 2 tbsp. apple vinegar (see p. 249)
- 1 ¾ cup (400 ml) grapeseed oil

Chipotle barbecue sauce
- 1 dried chipotle chili
- 3 tbsp. concentrated tomato puree
- 3 tbsp. apple vinegar
- 4 tbsp. muscovado sugar
- salt

Make your buns and mincemeat patties as described on pp. 234 and 165.

Cut the cabbage into fine strips. Peel and grate the carrots on the rough side of a grater. Put the cabbage and carrots into a sieve and sprinkle with 1 tbsp. of salt. Let stand for 1 hour so the vegetable mixture will collapse and begin to release some water.

Meanwhile, make the mayonnaise. Start by putting egg yolks and 1 tsp. of salt in a bowl. Whip the vinegar into the egg yolks. Now pour the grapeseed oil in gradually and very slowly while whipping constantly. When all the oil is absorbed, add salt and possibly a bit of extra vinegar to taste.

Clench the cabbage and grated carrot between your hands and squeeze out as much water as you can. Place the cabbage and carrot in the bowl with mayonnaise (or another bowl that's large enough). Mix it all together well. Add salt and possibly a bit more vinegar to taste.

Now make the chipotle barbecue sauce: Light the fire and let it burn to fire strength 5 (or use the fire you used to cook the mincemeat patties). Find a corner of the fire with no flames but a lot of smoke. Put the dried chili in a sieve and place it over the smoke. Smoke the chili for 5 minutes, moving it around a bit along the way so it doesn't burn. Remove the chili and chop it as finely as possible. Mix tomato puree, vinegar, and muscovado sugar. Add the finely chopped chili and season with salt.

Cut the burger buns into halves and spread with a generous layer of chipotle barbecue sauce. Place the mincemeat patties onto the buns and top with a large spoonful of coleslaw. Assemble the burgers and eat immediately—use your hands for goodness' sake!

SWEET

ÆBLESKIVER

"DANISH DONUTS"

Any

6–7

Æbleskiver pan,
cast-iron campfire pan

MAKES 16 PIECES

- 4 eggs
- 2 tbsp. sugar
- ½ cup (125 g) butter + more for the pan
- 1 tsp. ground cardamom
- zest of 1 lemon
- grains of 1 vanilla pod
- 2 cups (250 g) flour
- 1 ¼ cups (300 ml) milk
- ¾ cup (200 g) yogurt
- jam
- sugar

Light the fire and let it burn to embers.

Meanwhile, divide the eggs into yolks and whites and place these in separate bowls. Whisk the egg whites and sugar to a light meringue.

Melt the butter and add cardamom, lemon zest, and vanilla grains. Let the pan simmer slightly until you notice an enticing aroma. Add the melted butter and spices to the egg yolks little by little, constantly whipping until you have the texture of a light mayonnaise. With a dough scraper, gently fold the meringue into the yolks little by little, so you can retain as much air in the dough as possible. In another bowl, mix flour with milk and yogurt to form a smooth dough. Fold the egg mass into the dough a bit at a time.

Place the campfire pan over the embers and put your *æbleskiver* pan on top of it. In this way, you ensure a proper heat distribution, and that the donuts don't burn on the outside before they are cooked through. Put a dollop of butter in each of the pan's holes, and fill up each hole with dough. Allow the dough to bake a bit, then turn each donut upward a bit and add more dough. Bake again and turn the donuts a bit further upward. Finally, there is a hole in the top; fill with more dough, then turn the hole downward and bake a bit longer. This way you end up with donuts that are perfectly spherical and do not collapse when served (it also makes your donuts quite substantial, so you might need to lie down and rest after eating them!).

Serve with jam and sugar.

PINEAPPLE

WITH RUM & MUSCOVADO

Rakovalkea fire

3–4

Rotisserie or 1 skewer, 3 feet (1 m) long, 2 Y-shaped sticks

SERVES 6

- ¾ cup (170 g) muscovado sugar
- ½ cup (100 ml) dark rum
- 1 pineapple
- 2 cups (500 ml) whipping cream

Start by building your campfire. A *rakovalkea* fire will be a pain in the butt the first time you make one, so be prepared to spend some time getting it up and running.

Pour the sugar and rum into a saucepan and bring to a boil. It doesn't matter if the flames ignite the alcohol in the pan—it will evaporate sooner or later anyway. Let the liquid cook for a few minutes, until the consistency is slightly thicker than liquid honey. Take the pan off the heat.

Now prepare the pineapple. Peel it by running a knife from top to bottom, then following the "eyes" on the pineapple while holding the knife at an angle. Cut gently with the knife on each side of the pineapple's eyes so that you spiral around the fruit. Continue all the way around until you have removed all the eyes.

Put the pineapple on your skewer or place it on the rotisserie so that the pineapple is about 2 ¾–3 inches (7–10 cm) away from the flames. Rotate as you gradually pour the rum/sugar mixture over the pineapple, and let the glaze caramelize. Let the pineapple cook like this for about 1 hour.

Immediately before serving, whip the cream into a lightly whipped cream. Take the pineapple off the skewer, divide it into large pieces, spoon whipped cream over the pineapple pieces, and serve.

PANCAKES

Log cabin, lean-to, or hunter's fire

5–6

Cast-iron campfire pan

MAKES 10 PIECES

- ½ cup (100 g) butter
- 1½ cups (400 ml) whole milk
- 3 tbsp. sugar
- grains of 1 vanilla pod
- juice and zest of 1 orange
- juice and zest of 1 lemon
- 3 eggs
- ½ tsp. salt
- 1 cup (125 g) wheat flour
- more butter for frying

Light the fire and let it burn to embers.

Put the campfire pan over the fire and let it heat up well. Place a saucepan on the campfire pan and let the butter brown in it until the whey is golden and nutty in color. Pour the milk into the saucepan and remove from the heat. Add sugar, the grains from the vanilla pod, the juice and zest of both fruits, and the eggs and salt. Beat it all together until homogeneous. Add the flour a bit at a time while constantly stirring so that the batter does not clump together.

Place a regular (preferably cast-iron) pan on the campfire pan and let it get so hot that butter sizzles when it touches the pan. Let the butter melt and cover the bottom of the pan with a thin layer of pancake batter. Fry until golden on both sides and repeat until all the batter is used. Occasionally, give the batter a proper whip in the saucepan to create some foam. Make sure to pour a bit of the foam onto the pan with the batter—this will make the edges crispy.

If you are lucky enough to have a berry bush nearby, pick some berries and put them in the pancakes. They're also delicious served with ice cream or sugar.

WAFFLES

Log cabin, lean-to, or hunter's fire

5–7

Cast-iron waffle iron, grill rack

MAKES 6 PIECES

- 2 cups (250 g) flour
- 3 tbsp. sugar
- 1 tsp. salt
- 1 tsp. ground cardamom
- 1½ cups (350 ml) whole milk
- ½ cup (125 g) butter
- 3 eggs
- more butter for frying

The campfire lures the family out at all times of the year. Who doesn't like to sit around a glowing campfire? Our children take a little more persuading though, when grilled oysters and duck hearts are on the menu. But once that waffle iron comes out of the cupboard, they'll come racing toward the fire before you can say "waffles."

Light the fire and let it burn to embers.

Mix together flour, sugar, salt, and cardamom in a bowl, and stir in the milk. Melt the butter on low heat. Whip the eggs until airy in another bowl—the more air you whip into them, the fluffier your waffles will be. As you continue to whip, pour the melted butter into the airy eggs a bit at a time, as if you were making mayonnaise. When all the butter is absorbed, use a dough scraper to gently fold the egg and butter mixture together with the flour and milk mixture.

Place the grill rack about 4 inches (10 cm) above the embers of your fire. Put the waffle iron on the grill rack and let it heat through on both sides. Open the iron and add a spoonful of butter to melt. Turn the iron a few times so that the butter is evenly distributed.

Open the iron again and add a couple of tablespoons of waffle batter; how much depends on the size of your waffle iron. Close the waffle iron and leave it closed for 2 minutes. This is absolutely crucial if you want a fluffy waffle. Turn the iron around and let it heat from the other side for another 2 minutes.

Now open carefully and check if your waffle is done. If it is not yet golden, just close it again and fry for a bit longer.

FRENCH TOAST

"DRUNKEN KNIGHTS"

Log cabin, lean-to, or teepee fire

7–8

Grill rack, grill net

SERVES 4

For the syrup

- ½ cup (120 g) cane sugar
- ½ cup (100 ml) bourbon whiskey
- 2 pieces of cinnamon
- juice of ½ lemon
- 2 cups (500 ml) water

For the "knights"

- 1 small brioche
- 6 eggs
- ¼ cup (75 g) cane sugar
- 1 cup (250 ml) whipping cream
- 1 cup (250 ml) whole milk
- 3 tbsp. (50 ml) bourbon whiskey
- ½ nutmeg, grated

French toast is called arme riddere *("drunken knights") in Danish, so in my version I have added a bit of extra booze to make the toast even drunker.*
—Nicolai

Light the fire and let it burn to embers.

Start by making the whiskey-cinnamon syrup, as you want it to cool down a bit before serving. In a saucepan, add cane sugar, water, and half of the whiskey plus the 2 pieces of cinnamon. Cook on a grill rack over the embers until the caramel is golden. Remove the saucepan from the heat and add the remaining whiskey. Stir to mix. Stir the lemon juice into the syrup and add a bit of water if the texture is too thick. Set aside.

Cut the bread into 8 chunky slices. Whisk together eggs, sugar, cream, milk, and whiskey. Add grated nutmeg and whisk again.

Now dip each slice of brioche into the mixture and let it soak for a few minutes. Lift the bread up and let it drip slightly.

Place the pieces of bread in the grill net and grill until golden on each side by holding them over the embers.

Pour the whiskey syrup over the warm "knights." Serve and enjoy.

FIGS

WITH ROASTED OATMEAL

Log cabin, lean-to, or hunter's fire

5–6

Grill rack

SERVES 4

- 2 ½ oz. (75 g) butter
- 1 cup (150 g) coarsely rolled oatmeal
- ¼ cup (50 g) sugar
- ⅓ tsp. fine salt
- 3 tbsp. bitter olive oil
- 12 figs

These figs can be used to complement a strong blue cheese, or served with a scoop of vanilla ice cream as a dessert. They can also accompany French toast (see p. 215), or you can simply eat them just as they are.

Light the fire and let it burn to embers.

Melt the butter in a saucepan and add oatmeal, sugar, and salt. Let the oatmeal roast in the butter while stirring constantly. This should be done gently, so that the sugar caramelizes while the oatmeal roasts and turns golden. If needed, take the saucepan off the heat during the process so you don't risk burning it. When the grains are roasted, add olive oil, stir gently, and keep warm.

Place a grill rack over the embers. Cut the figs into halves and grill them until golden and caramelized. Place them with the cut side facing up, add roasted oatmeal, and finally pour over the juice from the bottom of the saucepan.

GRIDDLE CAKES

"KRABBELURER"

Swedish torch

6–7

MAKES 12 PIECES

- 2 eggs
- 2 tbsp. sugar
- 1 cup (300 ml) whole milk
- 1 cup (250 ml) wheat flour
- 1 tsp. baking powder
- 3 tbsp. (50 g) butter for frying
- 1 cup (100 g) raspberries
- 1 cup (100 g) blueberries
- 1 small bunch of mint
- more sugar as desired

Krabbelurer *is Swedish vernacular for a kind of thick pancake that the outdoorsy Swedes often cook over an open fire. I first encountered them when I accompanied my oldest son to a boy scout meeting, and I loved them instantly. So did our kids, needless to say. For this recipe, I used a Swedish torch, but you can easily use one of the other campfires as well, such as a log cabin fire.*
—Nicolai

Light the Swedish torch and allow the flames to settle.

Meanwhile, prepare the batter. Whisk eggs and 2 tbsp. of sugar until airy, add milk and stir together. Mix flour and baking powder and whisk together with the eggs and milk.

Sprinkle as much sugar as you think is appropriate. I put about 1 cup (200 g) out on a dish and turn raspberries, blueberries, and mint leaves in it.

Put a pan on the fire and let it heat through. Add the butter and let it sizzle. Use a tablespoon to drip the batter into the pan, and fry each cake golden on one side. Turn and fry until golden on the other side as well. Immediately place the griddle cakes in the dish with sugar and berries and flip them a few times so they are well covered with sugar.

Eat them by folding a *krabbelurer* like a taco with some berries and mint in the middle. This is not the traditional Swedish way, but it sure tastes good!

ÉPOISSES
IN EMBERS

Any

9

SERVES 4

- 1 Époisses (or another cheese in a wooden box)
- 1 loaf of whole wheat bread (e. g. the manitoba bread on p. 236)

This can hardly be called a recipe, but it is one of my favorites nonetheless. I'm sure you will feel the same way once you have tried it. Époisses is not the only kind of cheese you can use; any cheese in a wooden box will do.
—Nicolai

Light the fire and let it burn almost entirely out.

Take the cheese out of the box and sprinkle enough water on the box to make it wet. Put the cheese back into the box and place it in the embers. Now just wait for the cheese to melt.

Dip pieces of the bread in the cheese and eat immediately. It's not just okay to double-dip—it's a must!

HANGED PEARS

WITH BLUE CHEESE & WALNUTS

Log cabin, teepee, or lean-to fire

3–5

2 Y-shaped sticks about 3 feet (1 m) in length,
1 stick about 3 feet (1 m) in length,
cord, coarse-mesh sieve

SERVES 2

- 2 conference pears
- 3 ½ tbsp. (50 ml) maple syrup
- 1 oz. (30 g) walnuts
- 1 ¾ oz. (50 g) good blue cheese
- salt

Light the fire.

Hammer 2 Y-sticks into the ground with just under 3 ¼ feet (1 m) of distance between them. Place the other stick over them to create a small frame from which to hang your pears.

Halve and remove the core from each pear, make a small hole in the top, and pull a cord through. Hang the pears on the stick so they are about 1–1 ¼ feet (30–40 cm) above the fire. Give the pears a spin every now and then so they are evenly cooked all over.

Brush each pear with maple syrup along the way and check for tenderness by sticking them with a knife. They should cook for about 1 hour, so it may be necessary to feed your fire once with fresh firewood along the way.

Put the walnuts in the sieve and roast them over the embers for about 5 minutes, until crisp. When the pears are tender and golden, take them off the stick and place them on a platter. Pour a spoonful of maple syrup into the hole where the cores were and arrange with blue cheese and walnuts. Finally, sprinkle with a bit of salt, and serve.

BREAD &
ALL
THE REST

FLATBREAD

Log cabin, lean-to, or hunter's fire

5

Grill rack

MAKES 8 PIECES

- 1 heaping tbsp. (18 g) yeast
- 1 cup (200 ml) water
- 2 tbsp. Greek yogurt
- 2 tbsp. honey
- ½ tbsp. salt
- 2 ¾ cup (350 g) wheat flour type 00

In addition to being an amazing addition to most dishes, this flatbread can also be a convenient and inexpensive way to use up your leftovers or empty the vegetable drawer. We have very successfully looked into the refrigerator, uninspired and hungry, and turned yesterday's leftovers into wonderful dinners. Use the build-it-yourself principle and throw in whatever pickles, dressings, or other condiments you have on the table.

Stir the yeast into the water and add the other ingredients while stirring. This is a rustic and quickly made dough, so you don't have to knead it smooth for a long time—it should be mostly just tossed together. Let the dough rise for a few hours.

Meanwhile, light the fire and let it burn up to strength 5.

Place a pile of flour on a clean surface and pour the dough into it. Pour some flour on top. The dough is very soft and completely unmanageable otherwise. Pull a piece of the dough off and tap it flat between your hands. Hit and stretch it as best you can—a rolling pin will do more harm than good, as it beats the air out of the dough. Stretch until the dough is as thin as you can get it.

Grill your thin dough on the grill over direct heat. You will find that bubbles form at the top of the bread. Wait for this to happen before doing anything. When the underside of the bread has a nice color to it, turn it over and grill the other side.

BURGER BUNS

Log cabin or lean-to fire

7–8

Campfire stand, Dutch oven, ember shovel, barbecue tongs

MAKES 8 PIECES

- 2 tbsp. (30 g) butter
- 1 cup (300 ml) whole milk
- 4 tbsp. (50 g) yeast
- 2 tbsp. sugar
- 1 tbsp. salt
- 4 cups (500 g) wheat flour
- 2 eggs
- 1 tbsp. (10 g) sesame seeds

Light the fire and let it burn to calm embers.

Meanwhile, make the dough. Melt the butter and pour it into a bowl with the milk. Let the yeast dissolve in the milk and butter. Add sugar and salt, and knead in half of the flour. Add 1 egg and the remaining flour and knead for 5–10 minutes. Put a damp cloth over the bowl and allow the dough to rise for 1 hour.

Take the dough out of the bowl and divide it into 8 equal pieces. Shape the dough into buns and lightly flatten them. Butter a piece of baking paper on the table and place the buns on it. Let them rise for 30 minutes.

Now prepare your Dutch oven. Set up your campfire stand and hang your Dutch oven on it. Place a shovelful of embers under the pot and on the lid, and let it heat through for 15 minutes. Remove the lid and find the right temperature using this procedure: Sprinkle a bit of flour in the bottom of the pot. If it gets dark and burnt quickly, the pot is too hot. Use the barbecue tongs to remove some of the embers under the pot and then leave it hanging without a lid until the flour turns golden, without getting burned when you sprinkle it in. The size of your Dutch oven determines how many buns you can bake at a time. But they should bake for only about 15 minutes, so the process goes reasonably fast, even if you can't bake them all at once.

Cut out the baking paper the buns are lying on so that each bun has a small square. You should not start moving them without the paper, as they collapse easily. Brush the top of each with 1 beaten egg and sprinkle generously with the sesame seeds. Put the buns in the Dutch oven (they grow about 30% bigger when baking, so give them some space). Put the lid on and pour a shovelful of embers over it. Bake the buns for about 15 minutes. Lift the lid off the Dutch oven and take out the buns. Remove the baking paper from the bottom and allow them to cool off slightly before cutting them into halves.

MANITOBA BREAD

WITH MALT

Log cabin, lean-to, or hunter's fire

6–7

Mixer, campfire stand, Dutch oven with a minimum volume of 6 quarts (6 l)

MAKES 1 BREAD

- 1 heaping tbsp. (18 g) yeast
- 4 ½ oz. (125 g) sourdough starter
- 1 tbsp. malt syrup
- 2 tbsp. dark malt flour
- 1 cup (250 ml) water
- ½ cup (100 ml) dark beer
- 3 ¾ cups (450 g) Manitoba flour
- ½ oz. (15 g) salt
- sunflower oil

Manitoba is a type of flour that contains a lot of gluten and produces bread with a crispy crust and a soft crumb. You can experiment with other types of flour if you'd like. You will need a mixer to make this bread, as the dough is simply too soft to work with by hand.

Day 1: In your mixer, mix together yeast, sourdough starter, malt syrup, and malt flour with water and beer at a relatively low speed. Put a dough hook on the machine and set it at the highest speed, add the flour, and let it knead for 15–20 minutes or until the dough gathers in a slick lump around the hook. Add the salt and let the mixer run for another minute. Prepare a bowl with oil and pour the dough into the bowl. Refrigerate and allow to rise overnight.

Day 2: Light the fire and let it burn to fire strength 5. Put a campfire stand over the embers and hang the Dutch oven on it. Let the pot heat up for 20 minutes. Take the lid off the pot and sprinkle a layer of flour on the bottom. The flour should be dark but not burnt. If it burns, move the embers below to one side so the temperature drops slightly. Pour in the dough and sprinkle some flour on top. Put the lid on and take half of the embers and place them on top of the lid. Let the bread bake over the embers for 40 minutes. Carefully lift the lid and check the bread. It should sound hollow when you tap it and appear crisp on the crust. If it doesn't, let it bake a bit longer.

When the bread is done, take it out and eat it while it is warm. If you'd like a real treat, try dipping it in melted Époisses (see p. 223).

PIZZA BIANCA

Log cabin or lean-to fire

7–8

Pizza trowel, grill rack

MAKES 5 PIZZAS

Dough

- 1 ½ cups (350 ml) water
- 5 ¼ oz. (150 g) sourdough starter (or yogurt)
- 2 tbsp. (25 g) yeast
- 1 tbsp. salt
- 1 tbsp. sugar
- 5 cups (650 g) wheat flour type 00

Filling

- 1 potato
- olive oil
- salt and pepper
- 3 fresh mozzarella cheeses
- 5 ¼ oz. (150 g) ricotta cheese
- 1 handful of rosemary leaves
- ¼ cup (50 g) pitted olives

Now, I know this will never be a real pizza, but I guarantee it will taste great anyway. You can use the exact same technique to make a red pizza, but this one will always be my favorite.
—Nicolai

Start by making the dough. Heat up the water a bit and whisk the other ingredients, except the flour, into it.

Work the flour into the dough and knead (possibly with a mixer) until it appears smooth and supple. Put the dough into a greased bowl and place a cloth over it. Let it rise to 3 times its size (this takes about 1 ½ hours).

Meanwhile, light the fire and let it burn to embers. Place the grill rack so it has a distance of about 6–8 inches (15–20 cm) from the embers. Your campfire must not be too hot; if it is, the pizza will burn before the filling heats up.

Divide the pizza dough into 5 equal pieces and roll each of them into a ball. Let them rise a bit more while you prepare the potatoes. Cut the potatoes into ¼-inch (3-mm) thick slices with a mandoline or a very sharp knife, sprinkle them with olive oil, and season well on both sides with salt and pepper. Grill the potato slices until golden on each side and remove them from the heat.

Have all your ingredients for the pizza ready for the next step. The following should be done in one fluid motion: Pull and stretch the dough until it is as thin as you can get it. Place it directly on the grill and let it puff up, then flip it 90 degrees with the pizza trowel and grill it until golden. Turn the dough around and spread the mozzarella, ricotta, grilled potato slices, rosemary leaves, and olives over it. Sprinkle with olive oil and salt. Put the trowel under the pizza and turn it 90 degrees. Leave the trowel under the pizza so it “absorbs” some of the heat and allows the pizza to bake more evenly. When the bottom is crisp and golden and the filling is warm, serve the pizza immediately.

BREAD ON A STICK

Teepee fire | 3–4 | Camping knife

MAKES ABOUT 12 PIECES

- 1 ½ cups (350 ml) water
- 5 ¼ oz. (150 g) sourdough starter
- 2 tbsp. (25 g) yeast
- 1 tbsp. sugar
- 1 tbsp. salt
- 5 ½ cups (650 g) Manitoba flour

Bread on a stick is quite a campfire classic, but seldom do we have the patience to cook it all the way through. This is a dish that benefits hugely from a bit more patience and attention, so give it a try next time!

Light the fire.

Heat the water a bit over the flames and remove from the heat. Add sourdough, yeast, sugar, and salt to the water. Knead the flour in and continue to knead until the dough feels smooth and supple. Put a cloth over the bowl and allow the dough to rise for 1 hour.

Meanwhile, find a good stick for each twist-bread baker. The sticks should be about as thick as a thumb and decrease in thickness toward the tip. Remove about 6 inches (15 cm) of the bark around the tip on each stick with your knife.

Divide the dough into 12 pieces. Roll each piece out as a thin sausage—the thinner the better. This is most easily done by standing up, flouring your hands, and holding the dough between the palms while rubbing your hands back and forth. Grab a stick and start wrapping the dough around the bark-free part, starting from the thickest point. Wrap the dough tightly around the stick.

Now it is time to bake the bread. Each baker has one stick, which must be kept away from the flames and embers so that the bread is slowly baked. It should not happen quickly. You know that the distance is appropriate when you can hold your hand between the bread and the fire for 10 seconds without getting heat burn. Rotate the stick along the way while baking the bread for about 10–12 minutes. You can darken the bread to your liking by bringing it closer to the heat when it's almost done.

Remove the bread from the heat and let it rest for a couple of minutes before pulling it off the stick with a rotating motion.

CHESTNUTS

Log cabin, lean-to, or hunter's fire

6–7

Cast-iron campfire pan

SERVES 2–4

- 2 ¼ cups (300 g) chestnuts
- ½ cup (100 g) soft butter
- 1 tsp. flaky salt
- juice and zest of 1 lemon

It was one of the shortest days of the year: a stunningly beautiful December morning. The kids were at school, so it was just me, Nicolai, and the sunrise. The world is so quiet at that time of the year. We made coffee and grilled chestnuts over the fire while discussing the various current world events and the day's plans. Our neighbor and his dog stopped by, and as we shared a bowlful of roasted chestnuts together, the chimney sweeper pulled into the driveway, soon to be pottering around up on our roof. Mornings like these I sometimes feel like wrapping up and saving in my pocket to brighten up a gray day later down the line.
—Eva

Light the fire. When it is ready, put the campfire pan over the flames and heat well for about 5 minutes.

Make a small incision in each of the chestnuts. Whether you make a fancy cross or just one cut doesn't really matter. The main thing is to make a hole in the outer layer—otherwise there is a risk that the chestnuts will "explode." Stir the butter with salt, lemon juice, and lemon zest. Roast the chestnuts dry on the campfire pan for 10–15 minutes, flipping them every so often.

Serve warm as a snack with the lemon butter on the side.

QUALITY
GLASSWARE

APPLE VINEGAR

5-liter jar or a bowl

- 5 quarts (5 l) water
- 2 ½ cups (500 g) sugar
- 10–20 organic apples

I got this recipe from my mother-in-law, who gave me a 5-liter jar of it as a Christmas present. I love how my mother-in-law knows that this is the kind of present that will make me happy. I wonder what my brother would say if I gave him the same present for Christmas.
—Nicolai

Bring the water and sugar to a boil, take off the heat, and let cool completely. Cut the apples into quarters but don't remove the peel and core. It is important that your apples are organic because if they have been sprayed with pesticides, the bacteria on the peel is removed, and with them the possibility of making vinegar.

Pour the sugar water over the apples in a jar or bowl. Place a plate over the apples so that they are pressed down under the liquid.

Leave at room temperature for a minimum of 6 weeks; it will turn into vinegar. I usually wait around 10 weeks before I consider it ready.

ROSEHIP PETALS

PICKLED & AS VINEGAR

1-quart (1-liter)
mason jar

- 4 handfuls of rosehip petals
- 3 ¾ cups (900 ml) apple vinegar (see p. 249)

These pickled rosehip petals can be used in salads and as an aromatic acidic element for seafood dishes. The vinegar will be tasty and pink and can be used for vinaigrettes and for pickling other foods.

Pick the rosehip petals and brush them free of any bugs, but do not rinse them. Place the petals in the mason jar and pour the cold apple vinegar over them. Store in the refrigerator. The petals should steep in the vinegar for about 3 weeks before use, and preferably longer.

ELDERFLOWER

PICKLED & AS VINEGAR

1-quart (1-liter)
mason jar

- 12 elderflowers
- 3 ¾ cups (900 ml) apple vinegar (see p. 249)

When the elder trees are in bloom, it's time to pickle. Not only is it a joy to have elderflower vinegar on the kitchen shelf, but the flowers themselves taste wonderfully aromatic, and sour too, when they have been steeped in the apple vinegar for as long as possible. It's a real pleasure to bring out a rare dash of summer on a cold day by throwing a handful of pickled elderflowers on a salad or a plate of root vegetables. The vinegar can be used for vinaigrettes and for pickling other foods.

Pick the elderflowers and remove any bugs, but do not rinse them. Place in the mason jar and pour the cold apple vinegar over them. Store in the refrigerator. The elderflowers should steep in the vinegar for at least 6 weeks before use, and preferably longer.

PICKLED CHILIES

1-¼-cup (300-ml)
mason jar

- 1 large handful of chilies (as many as you can fit in the jar)
- 1 cup (250 ml) apple vinegar (see p. 249)

These pickled chilies work well as a spicy and acidic element to accompany vegetables, fish, and meat, and the vinegar can be used in vinaigrettes to add a spicy kick.

Puncture each chili with a fork and place them one by one in the mason jar. Pour the cold apple vinegar over them and let stand at room temperature for a minimum of 6 weeks, and preferably longer.

SMOKED BUTTER

Log cabin, teepee, or lean-to fire

5

Small fire tongs, 1 small jar

- 9 oz. (250 g) butter

This butter can be used in sauces, warm vinaigrettes, or anywhere you would like a nice, smoky taste. Go ahead and make an extra portion while you're at it. With a jar of smoked butter in the refrigerator, you always have the taste of the campfire at hand, even days when you don't have the time to light a fire.

Light the fire and let it burn to large embers.

Melt the butter and pour it into a saucepan or mason jar. Take a small piece of glowing firewood out of the fire with the tongs and immerse it in the butter so the flames go out and it starts to smoke. Cover and leave it for a few hours at room temperature. Skim the butter (if it has gotten cold, melt it gently) and pour it into a jar. Store in the refrigerator.

SALSA ROMESCO

Log cabin, lean-to, or hunter's fire

5–6

Blender, 1 jar

- 3 red bell peppers
- 1 shallot
- 2 cloves of garlic
- ½ cup (100 ml) olive oil
- ¾ cup (100 g) smoked almonds
- 3 tbsp. sherry vinegar
- salt

This recipe is a nod to an old boss of mine, chef Paulo Guimaraes, who introduced me to salsa romesco when I was a chef's apprentice. It has stayed with me ever since because there are virtually no savory dishes out there that aren't taken to another level with a spoonful of romesco on the side.
—Nicolai

Light the fire and let it burn to large flames.

Put the bell peppers directly into the embers and let them turn black all over. Now place the peppers in a small, lidded container such as a jar and close the lid. Leave them to steam in the container for about 5–10 minutes.

Remove the peppers from the container and remove the stems, seeds, and burnt skin. Use a blender to blend the peppers together with all the other ingredients. And voila! Your romesco is ready.

OUR PERSONAL STORY

NICOLAI

My campfire journey began in 2002 in Copenhagen, where I began training to become a chef. It was at a time when molecular gastronomy was at its peak. For the budding chef's apprentice I was, it felt like taking a sneak peek into the wizard's crystal ball as new techniques and dishes emerged from the likes of Ferran Adrià and Heston Blumenthal. Liquid nitrogen and hot gels seemed to dominate the gastronomic image of the future. It was magical, it was alluring, and I was swallowing it up whole. I had to know which magical powders and high-tech machines were used to produce these miracles, and this captivated me so much that I read and researched everything I could on the subject. To this day, I still know all kinds of molecular gastronomic techniques off the top of my head. For a long time, I felt as though I had found the culinary equivalent of the philosopher's stone. But what I didn't realize was that my eagerness to discover new culinary impossibilities was overshadowing what good cooking really is. Because, as you may already know, the best food is not made with whimsical techniques and mystery powder. The best food is made with love, thoughtfulness, quality ingredients, and a great sense of taste.

If I could rewind time and give the young chef's-apprentice-me some advice, I would advise him to be less preoccupied with the future and instead look backward and inward. I was training at Le Sommelier in Copenhagen under the head chef Francis Cardenau, who, with his classic French background, was among the pioneers who created a breeding ground for the high-level Nordic gastronomy we see today. At Le Sommelier, I learned to master the French style of cooking. But still, I could not muster the same fascination for the classic French cuisine as I had for the Spanish techno-emotional kitchen. So, as soon as I got my diploma, I went to Spain, where I worked at La Terraza del Casino: a Michelin 2-star restaurant in the El Bulli family. There, I learned to excel at the new Spanish cuisine's sacred tricks.

But despite my newfound expertise, I was still unaware of just how important the prerequisites of taste and love are if you want to cook something truly delicious. So when I lived out my dream of opening my own restaurant, it was short-lived. The concept—a Nordic bistro—was spot-on; the guests and the food critics loved it. But for me, every day was a struggle. I simply felt no joy behind the stove, only the mounting pressure of work. One morning, when I arrived at the restaurant and put my key in the door, I had a breakdown. Right then and there, I lost the desire to cook. I could not find any joy doing it, and perhaps it had never truly been there to begin with.

A few weeks later I met Eva, who later became my wonderful wife. Every morning I felt the sadness of leaving her to go to a job I simply did not enjoy. The combination of my blossoming relationship and my breakdown forced me to contemplate where I was in my life and what I really wanted. I wanted a family, and I did not want a job that dragged me down. I knew then that I didn't belong in the restaurant business, and that I would have to leave it behind me. I quit my job as head chef, handed the keys over to my partner, and left. Soon after, I was hired by Copenhagen Hospitality College to teach new chef's apprentices the craft. All those cooking theories I had absorbed over the years were being put to good use, and I had an amazing time.

Shortly after, I was offered a job at a TV production company. They wanted my help in launching the TV show *Masterchef* in Denmark. The contract of employment was three months to begin with, but I ended up working in the TV business for seven years. After working with *Masterchef* for three years, I was hired to develop new TV formats in all genres, and I was as far away from pots and pans as I could get. I fought a fierce battle to make people around me understand that I was no longer a cook, because I didn't feel like I was.

But gradually, something unexpected happened. It was shortly after we had the first of our two sons. Along with my new role as a family dad came a sudden desire to cook that I had not experienced before. When I made dinner for friends and family, rather than for paying guests, I suddenly found it inspiring, meditative, and fun. I was back on track, and although it seems strange looking back, I realize now that it was not until I was as far away from the cooking business as I could get that I actually came to love food. When the opportunity to create a new digital food channel appeared, it was as if almost everything fell into place. But I had to take one last step in order to complete the puzzle. A step that would prove to be the biggest, and one that would be taken with my wife.

Copenhagen 2016

We had ticked all the right boxes. We had two lovely kids, attractive jobs, a lovely home, and a relatively new car parked outside our apartment in one of Copenhagen's nicer residential neighborhoods. I had run the half-marathon mandatory for men my age. My wife had trained to become a sommelier. We had lovely neighbors and friends who came over for dinner for a few hours every now and then. On the weekends, we bundled the kids into the Christiania bike and cycled to the city's various parks and attractions such as aquariums, children's theatres, and playgrounds. Everything was so perfect in our little family. But behind that completed checklist of "things to achieve before turning 40" hid an everyday life that we weren't really enjoying as we should. We did not feel happy; we felt sedated.

The schedule was tightly planned. In the morning we dropped off our children at eight o'clock by the bus that would take them to the kindergarten on the outskirts of the city. Then we went off to our respective offices. Eight to nine hours later, we all met again, now completely stuffed full of processed information, thoughts, and other people's expectations. Cooking good food was a weekend thing; everyday food's value lay in how quickly and easily it could be made, as if it were an inconvenient speed bump in our fragmented lives. In our professional lives, food played a central role, but in our own nuclear family, it was not the natural focal point we felt it ought to be. Dinner was something we just had to get over with so that we could each escape to our respective corners of the couch and die a slow death with our phones or computers at hand. But before that, the kitchen had to be cleaned, the apartment tidied up, clothes folded, and the final emails answered, all before the day could repeat itself after a night's sleep that was usually just a little too short. We regularly looked at our bank account and wondered where the money we worked so hard for had gone. We exchanged wistful fantasies about journeying away from everyday life, but never felt like we had the money nor the time to act on them. We were hanging onto the edge of the cliff with our fingernails—or so it felt—and it became increasingly difficult to see each other. Our own life was making us nauseous.

The question continued creeping in, and in the end we could no longer ignore it: is this really the life we want?

Around this time, we came upon an opportunity to rent a house in Sweden cheaply. It was an old house from the 1860s situated in the middle of the woods. The plan was to have it as a holiday home. But every time we drove back to the city after spending weekends in that house, our children cried, and quite quickly the truth became clear to us adults, too: in fact, that house in the forest was our real home. This was the reason we left Copenhagen to settle down in the Swedish woodlands.

We had a dream of slowing down the pace, having more time to spend together as a family, more financial leeway, more time for better meals, and space for friends and family to come by for longer than just a couple of hours. But it was not just a romantic dream for us. It was simply necessary. I quit my job and started working from task to task, but only on things that made me happy. I began to focus more on what I had than what I wanted to achieve. It was in that state of mind that I really got hooked on fire.

Around the campfire, I noticed how the heat and flames could completely calm me down, sharpen my senses, and enhance my concentration. I became curious again—just as curious as I had been in cooking school. And in a way, I can say that I had become a student again. Only this time, the fire was my teacher. With the fire, I found the peace and tranquility I had subconsciously been looking for all my life. Along with the opportunity to be closer to nature and its changing seasons, it has truly given me the passion for food that I never found during my years as a chef.

Today, my hands are always dirty. They never were when I worked in the restaurant business. And if they had been, it's likely I would have been sacked. But soot and ash have settled in the little lines on my palms from my many hours spent around the fire. Hours I spent waiting, sensing, and taking my time. Today, I have made a conscious choice to cook how I cook. Cooking with the food instead of trying to squeeze it into a schedule. The process is far more satisfying and the result far tastier this way. The fire is my stove now. Tears roll down my cheeks because of the smoke in my eyes, I constantly walk around smelling like smoked sausage, and I love it!

Because, along with the quality produce and the care for the food and the people it is cooked for, I have found an equally important ingredient for better cooking: time.

—Nicolai Tram

EVA

My story is, in many ways, quite opposite to Nicolai's. I couldn't count how many summer evenings I spent around a smoking campfire in my childhood. And I have always loved to cook for family and friends. We lived by the sea, surrounded by woods and fields. My parents grew vegetables in the garden and bought local produce from the grocer and fresh fish from the fishmonger at the harbor. My childhood summer vacations were always in Sweden, where my parents cycled or paddled around in canoes for weeks on end, along with us kids. We went out in all kinds of weather, and usually we had the whole magnificent Swedish countryside to ourselves. I remember the magic of swimming in forest lakes, picking blueberries, and playing card games until late into the bright nights. I remember soaking up the sun on a rock on a hot summer day, and how we grilled trout over the campfire. But, to be honest, for many years it was the wet, rainy days of hauling my bike up endless steep hills that were most prominent in my memory.

When I was old enough to make my own decisions, I was drawn to the city, and for many years, I did all I could to avoid being in nature.

I was 18 when I moved to Nørrebro in central Copenhagen, where I lived on pasta, French fries, tap water, and canned beer. When I could afford a vacation, primitive bike and canoe trips were the last things on my mind. Instead, I went backpacking to exotic destinations, surrounded by people, parties, and guaranteed sunshine, or to exciting metropolises where I could soak in the buzz of the big city. Gastronomy became a strong interest of mine when I started working as a waitress alongside my studies in my early 20s. Gradually, the holidays became food journeys. I lived cheaply in a tiny apartment with a minimal kitchen. I rarely used it because I was basically never at home. When I was not studying, I was at work or going out, and tips and student loans were exchanged for dinners at fine dining restaurants in Europe's big cities and my hometown of Copenhagen.

I was intrigued by everything gastronomical: the techniques, the ingredients, the chefs, the waiters, the wines, the storytelling, the theater, and the opportunity to feel a bit like a princess. When I traveled, I always booked the cheapest hotel room I could possibly find within walking distance of the restaurants I wanted to visit, skipping museum visits and shopping sprees so that the money could be spent solely on what mattered: my great gastronomic experiences. I started a food blog with my sister and began documenting them.

When I graduated from the IT University of Copenhagen, my first real job was as a writer for online media, reporting news on the restaurant industry. I later started working as a freelance food critic, editor of a restaurant guide, and writer for food magazines. I wrote a steady stream of gastronomic trend stories, guides, chef profiles, and restaurant reviews. I had the exact job I had dreamed of in my early 20s. I would sit in fancy restaurants jotting down notes and taking photos for my blog. I managed to skip the 9-to-5 lifestyle when our children were quite young. I wanted the opportunity to choose my own working hours and projects, and to pick my kids up early. From the outside looking in, you'd think I'd found the sweet spot.

But even with flexible working hours, there are bills that have to be paid. It is expensive to be a family with children in Copenhagen. Every night that I wasn't going out for dinner at fancy restaurants, I was sitting behind the computer and writing for my job. Eventually, the magic aura that had surrounded gastronomy before disappeared for me. I would rather be with my family, but whenever I was, my thoughts were constantly roaming toward the computer and planning the next restaurant visits. There were deadlines approaching and people waiting for answers. I had the sinking feeling that the life we had created was not really a good fit for us. I could not express it back then, but today I can see what was missing: time for reflection and being present. I had a growing feeling that I had become a head mounted on a body I had no connection to.

After moving to the countryside, the pieces slowly began to fall into place. Living at a slower pace, with the opportunity to be in nature every day, meditation, exercise, and long hours around the fire, in the kitchen and at the dinner table, I gradually gained the ability to feel something again. I learned an incredible amount during that time. Among other things, I gained a new perspective on what kinds of food would bring me the greatest joy. Great food didn't have to mean something insanely delicious made by a celebrated chef whose restaurant had found its way into a guidebook or prestigious list (although, of course, that is also very nice). It could never compete with the joy I feel when cooking for family and friends, or when someone I love has poured their time, love, and careful attention into preparing a meal for me. To me, it is not a cliché to say that love is the most important ingredient. I have experienced in my own body how everyday stress and rushing through life can displace that love. So to me, today, it is essential that our family's meals are never—or at least extremely rarely—something that we rush through.

Living a good life is not about how many boxes you can tick. It's more about how you feel during the process. This became my mantra, and I decided I wanted to do more of what was doing me good. That is, cooking, being with family and friends, being in nature, and having a job that didn't tie me to a chair all day. It also meant pursuing a long-time dream I had never dared to act upon.

I first borrowed and later bought a camera and started photographing for real. Through the lens, I have regained my passion for food, only from a different angle this time. The camera has also allowed me to return to the magnificent Swedish nature I grew up with. To me, it's been like reuniting with an old flame, and every day I am stunned by how amazing nature truly is.

As you can imagine, it has been a dream come true for me make this book with my husband. Because nowhere do the joys of food, gastronomy, and nature go hand-in-hand more beautifully than when food is cooked with love over a glowing campfire.

Thank you very much for taking the time to read my story.

—Eva H. Tram

ABOUT THE AUTHORS

Eva and **Nicolai Tram** both come from careers in the gastronomic world and food media, she as a sommelier and food critic, he as a chef at fine dining restaurants and TV producer.

In 2017, they moved with their two young boys from the city of Copenhagen to the Swedish woods, seeking a better balance between work and family life.

As they spent more time in nature, they soon found that cooking on fire came naturally, and this book grew from their shared passion for cooking and nature.

After the original publication of *Cooking on Fire* in 2020, Nicolai and Eva Tram opened Knystaforsen, a restaurant with campfire cooking as the core of the kitchen. In 2022, the restaurant earned a Michelin star as well a Michelin green star for sustainability.

www.knystaforsen.se

Facebook/Instagram: @*knystaforsen*

INDEX

COOKING ON FIRE

Co-edited, texts, photography, and illustrations by Eva Helbæk Tram and Nicolai Tram

Edited by Robert Klanten

Copy-Editing by Marian Ryan

Design by Muusmann Forlag
Cover and layout by gestalten
Layout assistance by Tim Jonathan von Holst

Editorial Management by Arndt Jasper

Typefaces: Bliss Pro by Jeremy Tankard Typography, Steelworks by Eric Kurniawan

Printed by Tuijtel, Hardinxveld-Giessendam, Netherlands
Made in Europe

Published by gestalten, Berlin 2023
ISBN 978-3-96704-131-6

For more information, and to order books, please visit www.gestalten.com

Bibliographic information published by the Deutsche Nationalbibliothek.
The Deutsche Nationalbibliothek lists this publication in the Deutsche Nationalbibliografie; detailed bibliographic data is available online at www.dnb.de

This book was printed on paper certified according to the standards of the FSC®.

FSC www.fsc.org MIX Paper | Supporting responsible forestry FSC® C007225